THE PHOENIX EFFECT

9 Revitalizing Strategies
No Business Can
Do Without

CARTER PATE
HARLAN PLATT

John Wiley & Sons, Inc.

ISBN 0-471-06262-6

Printed in the United States of America.

10 9 8 7 6 5 4 3 2

To my wife, Angie, of 25 years,
and children, Justin, Chris, and David,
whose love makes this life worth living.

—*C.P.*

To Alex Alyokov, my undergraduate
honor's student at Northeastern
University, who renewed my thinking
on this book, and to other students
past and present.

—*H.P.*

CONTENTS

ACKNOWLEDGMENTS

In 1981, my young career as an acquisitions accountant took a turn that would forever change my life. I was asked to look into an acquisition that I had helped approve to see what had gone wrong. That investigation took me into a world of corporate crisis and renewal that would become the foundation of a lifelong career helping under-performing companies. Despite many years of excitement and challenges, I was always confronted with the same question posed to me year after year when shareholders, employees, and creditors alike asked "What went wrong, and what could we have done differently?"

My quest to help underperforming companies regain their glories of past years inspired me to join coauthor Harlan Platt to finally write the book that would answer that timeless question. Those lessons learned we call *The Phoenix Effect*. To take on a project of this magnitude, one has to surround oneself with the brightest people one can find in order to navigate the maze of difficulties one runs into trying to get raw ideas into a framework and then on paper. Harlan and I have tried to explain the amazing effect that companies benefit from when their future is at stake and they concentrate on the nine issues addressed in our book.

I need to thank Lisa Schaefer, who was vigilant on keeping us organized. PricewaterhouseCoopers has incredible people who watched over this whole process, and I would like to thank Joel Kurtzman, Martin Frimut, Roger Lipsey, Hilary Krane, Jason O'Neil, and Alexander Nolte, all who gave countless hours to this project. I am also forever grateful to Donna Carpenter and Maurice Coyle for allowing me the opportunity to learn from them the fine art of writing and of bringing a book to fruition. A special thank you goes to Helen Rees and Cindy Sammons of Wordworks for the terrific effort in pulling this all together, as well as John Wiley & Sons, Inc., for their willingness to publish our book.

There have been many mentors and friends along the way who each took precious time to help me at every step, and I fondly remember Larry Wright, Harold Abramson, Ray Ranelli, Philip Wright, Ed Siskin, Russ Munsch, Pat Neligan, Pastor Sam Dennis, Bob Medlin, Len Blackwell, Jack Stone, Otis Winters, Ben Landriscina, Dom DiNapoli, Freddie Reiss, David Williams, Delain Gray, Tom Codd, and, of course, my right arm for the last 11 years, Jo Cobb. Many times I have had an encouraging word from Jo just when I needed it.

I thank my father and mother, James H. "Buck" and Marjorie Pate, for the countless hours they invested in me, teaching me many of the life lessons and people skills that I use today.

—C.P.

Twenty years ago, I came to Northeastern University after having spent five years as a consultant. The economy at that time was weak, and companies all around were failing. Soon thereafter I posed a question to myself that I still cannot answer: Can you uncover a good manager working at a bad firm, and can you identify a bad manager working in a good firm? I have spent much of the last 20 years trying to answer that question. Although this book does not answer that question, it in part derives from that inquiry.

My search for answers was greatly aided in 1993 when the Turnaround Management Association asked me to be the faculty dean of its new certifying body, the Association of Certified Turnaround Professionals. During the past eight years, I have had the pleasure of working with some of the top turnaround and crisis managers in the country. They taught me a great deal.

Carter Pate and I met as a result of the certification program. Despite his stature in the industry and in his firm, he boldly volunteered to study for and to take the examination. Those who know Carter were not surprised when he soon passed the examination and became a certified turnaround professional, a CTP. Our working relationship evolved out of a mutual interest in seeing the work of the turnaround manager extended to include helping all companies, not just those in crisis. Carter and I saw the discipline as having broad applicability and value. This book represents our attempt to convey to all business managers, both the good and the bad, that a set of skills or strategies exists that will help them tune up, turnaround, or resolve the crisis in their business.

Without the assistance of several people, this project would have stumbled. Most notable are Donna Carpenter and Maurice Coyle, but also Lisa Schaefer at PricewaterhouseCoopers, and my secretaries Kathy Musker and Melissa Froio at Northeastern University. In addition, I would like to thank John Frabotta and Dick Omonhundro of Harborview Capital for their insights; Mike Segal, Henry Garelich, and Pierre Poulin for their many conversations; and my undergraduate, MBA, and high technology MBA students at Northeastern and my students in the Harvard University Extension Program for the many lessons they have taught me.

As with all things I have done, my wife, Marjorie, has set the standard and provided the encouragement.

—H.P.

INTRODUCTION

In Egyptian mythology, the fabled phoenix was a beautiful gold-and-purple male bird that lived in the desert for exactly 500 years and then immolated itself on a funeral pyre, whereupon another phoenix arose from the ashes and the cycle was repeated, over and over. Connected with sun worship (as in the sun's daily rebirth), the phoenix myth later became a Greek version of immortality and eventually a Christian allegory mirroring the resurrection. As a unique symbol of renewal, of rising from the ashes, the phoenix has since appealed to everyone from medieval alchemists (hence the sign over pharmacies) to Britain's World War II commandos (who wore the phoenix insignia) to James Joyce (whose masterpiece, *Finnegans Wake*, depicts Dublin's Phoenix Park as the Garden of Eden).

We the authors of *The Phoenix Effect* are no Joyces, but as specialists in the fine art of restructuring underperforming companies, we yield to no one in admiring the phoenix, the quintessential comeback kid. It stands for our business: transforming your company. Using the methods and precedents we have laid out in this book, virtually any organization can revitalize itself and thrive again in the style to which it should be accustomed.

This is a large claim to which we bring the pooled experience of a seasoned field operative and a leading academic, both armed with commensurate credentials. Carter Pate is the partner responsible for PricewaterhouseCoopers LLP's Financial Advisory Services (FAS) in the Americas theater and a member of the Corporate Finance & Recovery Services Global Leadership Team. FAS-Americas employs more than 1,400 professionals in four product groups, which include Business Recovery Services (BRS); Dispute Analysis & Investigations; Real Estate; and Hospitality and Leisure. Mr. Pate, prior to his current position, was the U.S. product leader of Business Regeneration Services of PricewaterhouseCoopers LLP.

Harlan Platt is a professor of finance at Northeastern University in Boston, a director of the Debt Strategy Fund, and the author of four other books, including *Principles of Corporate Renewal.* Dr. Platt created and now administers the certification exam for the Turnaround Management Association, the test that turnaround specialists take after gaining five years of experience.

The Phoenix Effect is a highly distilled concentrate of our diverse perspectives on business renewal issues and methods. We have boiled two lifetimes of experience into nine pivotal principles that we believe must be applied to revive any business. We urge you to put them to work in your business.

CHAPTER 1

Get to the Point of Pain

For a while, it looked as though Neostar, Inc., knew all the answers. In 1996, the Texas-based company built a chain of retail stores, located primarily in malls, specializing in computer software and the popular game cartridges about dragons, kingdoms, and adventures produced by the world's top suppliers. As business boomed, Neostar's leaders dreamt of building an empire of their own, and they bought other retail software stores. They also invested millions in a state-of-the-art distribution center.

Then everything went wrong. Customers, under ever more time pressure, abandoned older malls in favor of strip shopping centers, leaving all those Neostar outlets stuck in long-term mall leases. Internet-related products put personal computer software under pressure , and sales flagged. Meanwhile, the debt burden the company had taken on in its acquisition spree began to weigh heavily. Watching all these events with their customary acumen, the credit managers started refusing to ship their hot new games to Neostar until the company caught up with its receivables.

That was when its bankers group, concerned about its loans to the company, called on PricewaterhouseCoopers to take a close look at Neostar and determine what was needed to turn the business around.

As you will see in the pages ahead, this book is all about corporate renewal, or what we call the Phoenix Effect. We are both, in our separate ways, experts in the topic. Carter Pate is in charge of Financial Advisory Services at Price-waterhouseCoopers and has been involved in a number of the major corporate restructurings that firm has handled over the last five years. Harlan Platt, on the other hand, is a professor of finance at Northeastern University in Boston. He started the Association of Certified Turn-around Professional's, the national program that certifies turnaround managers, and with his company, 911Risk, Inc., develops models to predict financial distress.

Based on our experience and our studies, we have developed the Phoenix Effect, a new and practical approach to the corporate renewal process. We have, in this book, set forth nine strategies you can follow to confront, comprehend, and conquer your company's ills, big and small. We describe these steps in brief in this chapter, and in detail later on. And in each case, we offer examples from real life—case histories of companies that have sought to improve their performance by following one or another of these steps. You can benefit by their example.

It will make a significant difference, of course, how much your company's performance needs to improve. We divide organizations into three main categories—as Hollywood might put it, the good, the bad, and the ugly. Good companies dominate their markets. Bad ones have problems that can still be fixed. Ugly companies tremble at the edge of the abyss.

But all three kinds of businesses can gain by following our Phoenix Effect program. Good companies can become great companies with a tune-up; troubled ones can straighten out with a turnaround; and crisis management can enable the ugly to snatch success from the jaws of failure. Moreover, our program can be successfully applied in any industry by any business, large or small.

The first step of our nine is simple and direct: Get to the point of pain. In many ways, the job of the turnaround manager is comparable to that of the physician. The first task is to diagnose the corporate patient's condition before you can make the right prescription. Find out what hurts. In our model, that means deciding whether the problem is of a nature to call for a tune-up, a turnaround, or crisis management.

In the case of Neostar, the banks called us in because Neostar had informed them that it was in technical default of its loan agreements, which often contain clauses specifying certain inventory ratios and levels of working capital. Given the drop in revenues, the chief financial officer was no longer able—or willing—to sign the routine paperwork certifying that the company was in conformity with its loan covenants without exposing himself to personal liability.

So we knew something was wrong, but we had no idea just what it was.

Deciphering company health is not easy. Business analysts have always yearned for a magic formula that could evaluate any organization, however complex, and then describe its condition with a single number. No such formula will ever exist. The reality is that companies sometimes fly blindly all over the business world. Some poorly managed companies find ignorance perfectly acceptable—as long as they can meet next month's payroll. Others monitor elaborate measuring systems whose metrics supposedly tell all but seldom tell enough to eliminate human mischief, error, or folly.

How well a company is doing is often invisible. Two familiar bogeys—denial and deception—play their dissembling parts. In December 1997, Henry Silverman assembled a stable of companies including Avis, Days Inn, and Coldwell Banker. He called it Cendant Corporation: a $14 billion marketing giant eager for world business conquest. Four months later, the Cendant empire collapsed under the weight of a $200 million accounting error and a $500 million accounting dispute.

Our first step with Neostar, as with every client, was to do our homework before even contacting the company. We study all the public information we can find so we can ask intelligent questions. We read the 10K, the 10Q, and the 8K (documents that public companies are required to file with the Securities and Exchange Commission). We also talk to all the financial analysts who follow the company and read their reports.

Quite often, we go online. If your company has more than a thousand employees, there's a good chance it has created its own Web site, and what it has to say there can be most interesting to a questing consultant. Even more intriguing are the chat rooms created by disgruntled employees. The angrier sites are called things like XYZCompanyStinks.com (or worse). Probably half these people are furious because they just lost their jobs. But their conversations provide us with insights about the true state of the organization that we may not hear from management.

You can learn a lot that way, but we make sure that we keep an open mind about the company and are ready to modify our ideas in the face of new information. Inevitably, additional information arrives, but only after we get the top person to help us in our inside-the-company explorations. Sometimes it's the CEO, sometimes the president, but the point is to go right to the top, to the individual with final decision-making power. The top person needs to be convinced that you are acting in his or her best interest. After all, if improvements aren't made, the chief executive is often the first to go.

Over the years, we have learned not to rush into the relationship with the CEO, proudly informing him or her as to how smart we are about the company. We exercise restraint in that regard, and we never offer an opinion about a client organization's problems during our first few days there. We are there to listen and observe and not to irritate the chief executive by pontificating. As the old adage says, "It's better to remain silent and be thought a fool than to open your mouth and remove all doubt."

What we actually say is something like this: "We've had a chance to read your 10K, your 10Q, your 8K. We've looked at a number of financial analysts' reports. And we've read some odd stories that apparently a few of your employees—obviously disgruntled—have posted on the Internet. It's all pretty complex. Now, could you share your own perception of what it is about this company that keeps you awake at night?"

Most of the managers we have met don't read every word of the formal, official reports their companies are required to submit. So they immediately wonder what we know, or what adverse information we've picked up on the Internet. Do we know the real story of why the company missed last year's earnings? Do we know about that grim problem in the Savannah plant?

At which point, utterly warm and supportive, and after a long pause to let the situation sink in, we say again, "So why don't you tell us what's really going on?"

Most often, that kind of approach will lead people to open up, often with a rush of words. Now the conversation gets interesting. They say things like, "Look, we've run out of cash, period." Or: "I launched three new products last year; they all failed. The board is telling me I'll be gone in six weeks if I don't come up with a fix right now."

Such answers, of course, are never enough. Besieged leaders see an effect, but not what is causing it. They can't seem to diagnose the problem. It's awful to see one of these people in pain, even shattered by a sudden loss of confidence. Yesterday, master of the universe; today, hopelessly overwhelmed.

At this stage, the questions must be narrowly aimed at identifying the immediate problem. We don't dwell on side issues—we skip all the problems of marketing, manufacturing, and strategy. Those are for later when we have more leisure to think long and big. Right now, it's down-and-dirty time. Get to the point of pain.

Has any law been broken?

Has there been an embezzlement?

Have any taxes not been paid or withheld? Any problems with the Internal Revenue Service?

Are any lawsuits threatening the company's viability and causing people on the outside to be wary?

Has there been a tender offer for this company that we don't know about?

Finally, and most immediately crucial: What exactly is your cash position?

We would hate to spend a week talking strategy and then have the controller suddenly find his voice and tell us, "By the way, I am not sure we can make payroll next month." We would look like novices if we didn't check on cash flow the first day we arrived. Remember, we are there to improve performance; the faster we can find out what we need to find out, the greater the chance of success.

In the case of Neostar, the top man we talked with assured us initially that the problem was minor and short-lived, and that he and his team were on top of it. We weren't so sure of that, but we said nothing and did a cash flow statement. The results were horrendous. We will never forget the look on the president's face when we informed him, "You won't be able to make payroll in eight weeks." He was flabbergasted. His people hadn't been telling him the bad news he needed to know. It was as though he had been awakened in the middle of the night to discover that he was sleeping in the wrong house.

It is a familiar quandary. As a manager, you want to be sure that your aides don't get into the habit of laying every problem on your desk and expecting you to solve it. They have to learn to take responsibility. You also don't want them to hesitate to bring you important downside data. If you make it miserable for them to be the bearers of bad tidings, they will find ways to steer clear of you.

Typically, the manager tells the CEO that he has had to struggle to meet payroll, and the CEO says, "Handle it." When the same thing happens several more times, and the CEO offers the same response, louder and angrier each time, the manager keeps the bad news to himself for a few months. Then, when he announces, "I can't make payroll this month," the CEO says, "How in the world could this happen? Why didn't you warn me?"

You will recall that we earlier identified three kinds of companies—the good, the bad, and the ugly. Neostar's circumstances were ugly indeed. The consumers' move away from malls meant that the company's stores no longer attracted the volume of customer traffic necessary to meet its sales goals. The advent of the Internet and the replication of disk technology cut into its revenues. The expensive distribution center weighed down profits. Working capital plummeted.

It was clear that Neostar needed more than a tune-up or a turnaround; it would require crisis management. Later on, we describe just how we went about that. Suffice it to say here that our priority in such instances is to keep these faltering companies solvent. When failure looms, drastic measures are taken to guide companies through bankruptcy or liquidation. Correctly applied, they can turn a lemon into lemon meringue pie, bringing seemingly moribund organizations back to vigorous life.

When good businesses seek our help, the process we apply is more one of tune-up management. We urge them to confront themselves with tough, irreverent questions like "What are we doing wrong?" and "What can we do better?" In other words, how can we help a strong company get stronger?

Turnaround management is the term we use for helping companies with modest problems. Drawing on business tools from accounting, finance, and marketing, a turnaround team solves specific problems that hold back a business but do not threaten its survival. The process generates improvements that can turn a market laggard into a market leader.

One trait the three types of companies have in common is the manner in which they usually come to our attention. Almost never does a president or chief executive call with anything but a minor complaint. It usually takes time before he or she understands—or admits—the gravity of the situation. As we pointed out earlier, that takes patience.

Table 1.1 shows another way of thinking about our first step toward putting the Phoenix Effect to work for you—determining which of the three company types best fits your circumstance. We have posed a series of all-to-familiar general business questions and positioned them according to appropriate company type.

In our new, reality-tested formula for corporate renewal, we use the same nine steps in treating all three of the company types, but, of course, the emphasis varies with the different circumstances. Tune-ups concentrate on strategic solutions, though they can also encompass financial and operating revisions. Turnarounds emphasize financial and operating adjustments, but strategy may be modified as well. Crisis resolution demands immediate financial changes, but operating changes may be added if time permits.

Now, here is a quick look at the nine steps, which correspond to the 10 chapters of this book.

TABLE 1.1 Questions to Help Evaluate Company
Performance

Tune-up	Turnaround	Crisis
Have earnings declined during the past three quarters?	Are you losing money now after years of being profitable?	Is payroll a problem?
Are there signs that sales may be leveling off?	Are your warehouses stuffed with unsold products?	Will your bank lend you more money?
Is your workforce as inspired as it used to be?	Are you having trouble recruiting new help?	Have your best employees quit?
Are your stock options still a valuable currency?	Are your partners trying to unload their equity on you?	Have some vendors stopped their shipments of goods to you?
Are you satisfied with results achieved in your last acquisition, product introduction, or market extension?	Do you know why you sell the products that you do in the markets that you are in?	Have you had a moment to think/strategize this week?
Have you developed a plan to maintain your excellent rate of growth in spite of new competitors entering the market?	Have competitors taken business away from you?	Have even the customers who don't pay stopped ordering from you?

1. Get to the Point of Pain

Finding out whether the business requires a tune-up, a turnaround, or crisis measures is the topic of this chapter.

2. Determine the Scope

Scope is the range of businesses and locations in which an organization operates. Some companies take on more than they can handle; others take on too little. Either mistake can be costly. In this chapter, we tell how to do it just right and provide case histories of businesses that sought that goal, successfully and unsuccessfully. We also discuss the advantages and disadvantages of the three possible decisions managers can make about a company's scope, namely, to stay in the same business, withdraw from an existing business, or enter a new one.

3. Orient the Business

In a crowded marketplace, it is crucial for businesses to use orientation to differentiate their products or services. Orientation is often found in mission statements: "We will deliver the best...lowest-cost...longest-lasting... safest...most environmentally friendly...product/service." The Phoenix Effect helps companies live up to their mission statements. We show in this chapter how companies have used orientation to define other aspects of the organization. For example, an enterprise that is oriented to deliver its product or service at the lowest cost will also tightly control labor costs and pursue importing and outsourcing opportunities.

4. Manage Scale

Bigness may or may not produce economies of scale. When successful businesses expand, they usually see a decrease in their costs for advertising, hiring, investing, purchasing, supervising, researching, managing, and more. But other growing companies watch their costs climb as well—a sure sign of trouble ahead. With practical advice and analysis of corporate examples, we help you decide whether your enterprise should grow, stay the same size, or shrink.

5. Handle Debt

Start with a thorough review of debt obligations and contracts. If it turns out that your business has excessive debt, you may find relief in equity-for-debt swaps, relaxed debt covenants, and asset exchanges in lieu of debt payments. Other areas to pursue include overpayments to unions, vendors, and executives, among others. Negotiating more favorable terms to relieve an organization's debt and obligations is a critical skill. This chapter includes a primer on negotiation that can help you maintain control in face-to-face meetings.

6. Get the Most from Assets

In this chapter, we assist you in scrutinizing your working capital to identify superfluous and underused assets. In the process, we show how to evaluate cost-saving and capital-raising opportunities that have short-term benefits—dismissing fewer employees, reducing inventories, and securing funding from suppliers, for example—but long-term downsides.

7. Get the Most from Employees

In this wide-ranging chapter, we offer ideas and suggestions for increasing the quality and productivity of your most important assets. Of course, they are among your most expensive assets as well. We place substantial emphasis on lowering costs related to the workforce and increasing output.

8. Get the Most from Products

Directly or indirectly, every product and customer should yield a profit. In this chapter, we aid you in making decisions about which products to sell, what customers to keep, and how to set prices. Successful corporate renewal programs usually focus early on turning out products that are consistently developed and marketed to fill actual, current customer needs.

9. Produce the Product

Here we consider and analyze the alternative ways products can be created, including owned or leased facilities (domestic or foreign), plantless production (outsourcing), and just-in-time (JIT) production. Does the factory serve the needs of the product? If not, what must be changed in order to make products faster, less expensive, or more consistent? Should operations be combined with those of another company or even a competitor?

10. Change the Process

The last step, and final chapter, is dedicated to one of the least expensive yet most frequently overlooked weapons in the corporate renewal armory: altering the functional processes of a business. Ordinary process improvements are cheap, fast, and sometimes ideal in turnaround or crisis resolution situations. Implementing them takes nothing more than a careful eye and determination. Unlike the comprehensive modifications that are part of reengineering, such ordinary changes involve simple transitions from less efficient to more efficient methods. The payoff can be huge.

By the time we had completed the first of the nine strategies with the people at Neostar, we realized that "crisis" was perhaps too mild a word to describe their company's circumstances. It was too late for anything but bankruptcy.

Still, all was not lost. There was a potential savior in the wings, a major Neostar shareholder named Leonard "Len" Riggio, who is the founder, chairman, and chief executive officer of Barnes & Noble, Inc., the number one bookseller in the United States. He was still high on the Neostar concept and ready to give it further financial support if the circumstances were right. Together with Len, we developed a strategy to bring about those circumstances. Using the nine strategies we have described, we found ways to bring Neostar back to life. Among them:

- *Size.* With the help of the bankruptcy court, we closed down about half of the existing Neostar stores. The goal was to return the company to what had been its successful core operation. The economies-of-scale strategy had never really worked.

■ *Assets.* We were using payables as a source of working capital, but Nintendo got tired of waiting for its money, so we ended up giving the company cash up front for its product.

■ *Employees.* In shrinking the size of the operation, we cherry-picked managers who would stay with the company to make sure we got the most from the remaining employees.

At the end of the bankruptcy process, Len discovered that he had to bid against a Neostar competitor for the stores that remained. We advised him to make a relatively low cash offer, balancing it with a plan that would keep many more employees working than would the opposing arrangement. We proved to the judge that the claims against the estate lodged by the greater number of discharged employees would far exceed the difference between the cash offers.

Len, a terrific talent, succeeded in the end, bringing the organization out of bankruptcy. Within six months after leaving bankruptcy, the reborn Neostar, having implemented many of our suggested strategies, was posting a profit.

How You're Doing Is Where You're Going

Why one company grows and another dies is a question with as many answers as there are businesses. But if there is one fundamental source of life in companies, as in people, it is the capacity for self-renewal, the ability to excite your team for game after game, to inspire your players to go for broke season after season.

Where does that ability come from? Genetics, charisma, sheer luck, stock options—all crucial, yes, but the best renewal insurance is a leader who always knows exactly how his or her company is doing. This leader never dwells on past glory, the siren call of complacency. He or she is a master of today's vital signs, the indicators of tomorrow's success or failure. This leader is forever poking around the ship's innards and surfaces, as alert to its creaks and groans as a seabird is to wind and waves. Best of all, this leader is a pragmatist as well as an artist, an insatiable demander and consumer of critical data.

The key insight of our profession is that companies are seldom what they think they are. The strong overlook their flaws; the weak overlook their possibilities. The abyss yawns for both, but it need not. By constantly examining real-time data, using our simple methodology, the leaders of both strong and weak companies can set realistic goals and achieve them year after year after year.

In the pages ahead, you will find detailed proof of that contention: examples of organizations that have followed our Phoenix Effect program and, indeed, renewed their energy, productivity, and profitability. In the next chapter, we explain how you can determine your company's optimum scope.

CHAPTER 2

Determine the Scope

Big or small, every business has scope—that is, the range of its ambitions, opportunities, and markets. Scope measures the extent of a corporation's businesses and locations. The corner deli's is tiny; the General Electric Company's is cosmic. Finding the range that best suits your organization's resources is critical. If some businesses have too much scope, others don't have enough. Either mistake is costly.

Leaders can move in three different directions when it comes to managing their company's scope: One, they can enter a new business, or broaden their scope; two, they can withdraw from an existing business, or narrow their scope; or three, they can stay in the same business, or maintain their scope.

The first option is the one we recommended to Tidel Engineering, Inc., a small manufacturer based in Carrollton, Texas.

In 1993, Tidel was dying of its own success. The company made excellent drop safes, the kind used in 7-Elevens and other high-volume stores. Tidel's selling point was that its safes foiled holdups: They were time-delayed, forcing robbers to wait between 5 and 10 long minutes before they had access to large amounts of money. Most thieves panicked and fled empty-handed.

Tidel's safes eventually saturated the market. Unfortunately, sales then plunged. The safes were so well made that no one needed replacements, and repairing old ones was less expensive than buying new ones. Worse, Tidel had neither plans nor capital to launch an alternative product. The company's cash dried up, it stopped paying its creditors, and it owed its bank $40 million, which might as well have been $40 billion.

This is the point at which coauthor Carter Pate was named the company's interim president and chief executive officer. His words describe what happened next.

When my team arrived, the owner was trying to hang on. He begged the bank to fund his payroll, but it refused. Fed up, he sent everyone home, locked the doors, and left town.

As the bankers saw it, the situation was desperate—a shut plant with exorbitant debts, no capital, and no product plans, and not even a workforce. It appeared to be a total loss.

However, we saw Tidel as a possible opportunity. We let its bankers know that $3 million was needed to restart the company. Though concerned about the chances for success, they seized the company's stock and installed me as interim president and CEO.

When I took a good hard look at all the possibilities, I kept scope foremost in my mind. I then asked my associate Len Blackwell to completely overhaul the manufacturing process. The fellow in manufacturing was a genius. Within four months, Len had completely redesigned the entire process, and Tidel Engineering was humming again with orders for redesigned old products and plans for a new product.

It was apparent that Tidel made excellent safes; the challenge was leveraging that competency to come up with a new product—that is, how to expand Tidel's scope.

How did we do it? We solved short-term needs by filling back orders that gave us the breathing room to launch new models. This, in turn, gave us time to redesign the drop-in safe to give it a whole new function as an automated teller machine. Now, it was an ATM in the old safe jacket.

Twelve months later, business was so good that we not only recovered $22 million for the bank, we also sold the company for $10 million.

We regard Tidel's return from the dead as a well-engineered scope transformation. Of course, other activities, including a restructuring of the company's debt, had to be tended to, but our decision to change the scope of Tidel's business was the critical rejuvenating factor.

In this chapter, we examine how several quite different companies have dealt with scope, both successfully and unsuccessfully, and we discuss the advantages and disadvantages of the various options: expanding, limiting, and maintaining scope. These are solid lessons for managers in any industry.

Determining Direction

The first step in managing scope is to determine which direction to take, then how far you can safely and profitably move. Most businesses reach a point at which they want to seek out new markets and new growth opportunities. Usually, this is because they are doing well, but sometimes, as in the case of Tidel, it is because they are in bad shape and need a life preserver. In either case, a company should look for the opportunities that fit its strategy, competencies, and culture.

How does an organization go about doing this?

In Texas, there is an old saying that it doesn't take a genius to spot a goat in a flock of sheep. When we study a company and talk to its employees, we watch for the goat—something that is out of place or doesn't quite fit. We like to talk to people below the top level—of course, you learn a lot from the CEO and CFO, but those a little further down the ladder often have very different perspectives, especially on the subject of scope. They have a real sense of where the organization is underextended.

There is another old saying in Texas: Always drink upstream from the herd. Some of the information that comes downstream is polluted or diluted. Also, you have to make sure that what you are hearing hasn't been contaminated—that is, altered by spin control. Say you hear that margins are down. The obvious conclusion would be that pricing is wrong or that manufacturing is too expensive. But by broadening your investigation and talking to the salespeople in the field, whose perspectives are very different from the chief financial officer's, you might realize that a market dynamic is changing and affecting margins in the process. They may know, for example, that the market has moved beyond the company's product, meaning that it is obsolete. And they are hearing that directly from customers.

We have found, too, that many people get wrapped up in internal data and ignore the market as a whole, which makes assessing scope impossible. You can't determine where to go until you know where you are.

The first action to take is to spend a day or two talking to people up and down the corporate food chain. Define where the challenges are; interview anyone and everyone so you can put together a picture of what is going on, and don't precipitously end these conversations. Listening can be an invaluable business tool. You never know who will have something worthwhile to say.

Listen to what people aren't telling you; it may be just as important as what they are. If you ask someone's opinion of a key product and get a carefully phrased, tangential answer, you can be sure there is more there than meets the ear.

Common sense will rarely steer you wrong. People love to tell you what is going wrong. Almost everyone has heard a story of an organization that overlooked the obvious and ended up deep in a hole. Here's another.

The evangelist Oral Roberts raised millions of dollars to build a state-of-the art cancer hospital and research center in Tulsa, Oklahoma. His vision was to draw people from around the world to be healed in his facility that merged the powers of medicine and prayer. With his advisers, he commissioned numerous studies of patient expectations and best hospital practices, while, at the same time, they combed the United States and the world for the most esteemed physicians. The result was a magnificent health care institution with a superb medical staff.

Yet, only months after it opened, the center was considered a failure and portions were shut down because a tremendously important point that speaks directly to scope was overlooked in the planning. When people are sick, they want to be near their families, and, for many, Tulsa was inconvenient. So, instead of reaching globally, Oral Roberts's cancer center had a patient base that was limited to about a 100-mile radius—not a large enough area to sustain a hospital this size in a city as large as Tulsa.

Had Roberts's advisers visited other cancer centers in Atlanta, Georgia; Boston, Massachusetts; or Seattle, Washington; for example, and asked the patients if they would be inclined to travel to Tulsa for treatment, they may have averted a costly miscalculation. It was a painful lesson about the limits of scope.

Factors That Affect Scope Decisions

Five "outside" factors that can profoundly influence a company's ability to grow should be considered when investigating scope. Let's take them each in turn.

The Big Picture

Is the economy in a downturn, on an upswing, or basically static? Is capital readily available? In what direction are interest rates moving? What do key economic indicators tell you? These trends are likely to have an impact on your business both now and in the long term. For example, as 2000 came to an end, Palm, Inc., based in Santa Clara, California, added new products to extend its line of personal digital assistants (PDAs) at both the high and low ends. But the company had an unpleasant awakening when a sharp decline in economic activity caused its products to remain on store shelves and in warehouses. As a result, Palm's stock price and product prices were impacted and employees were laid off.

The Competitive Landscape

Has the competition changed, or is it changing? Is obsolescence a threat? Is a dynamic upheaval shaking the market? Is a feisty new kid on the block or an established competitor getting ready to launch a new product? Analyzing your competitors' current scope and evaluating their future is essential to understanding your own. For example, *Wonder Boys,* a superb film that opened in February 2000, languished at the box office despite nearly unanimous critical acclaim (it appeared on more than 100 top movie lists). One problem was that the movie opened the same week as *The Whole Nine Yards,* a hugely successful film starring Bruce Willis and Matthew Perry. Worse, the advertising campaign for *Wonder Boys* failed to distinguish it from its competitors. Yet, driven by its overwhelming critical endorsements, Viacom, Inc.'s Paramount Pictures agreed to rerelease the film in November 2000 following a new marketing effort.

Social Change

Trends, fashions, and popular culture all have enormous impact on consumers' buying habits. For example, since most public places ban smoking, branching out into high-end ashtrays would be a terrible idea. Another similar example is swimming pools, which are no longer the sine qua non of a well-dressed suburban backyard, at least in some parts of the country. For example, in at least one state in 2000, more pools were removed than were built. Many families there have neither the time nor the inclination to take care of them or pay to have them maintained. Also, an unattended pool poses a dangerous temptation for little children who don't yet know how to swim. Our advice, then, is to keep a keen eye on the material culture, and you will find many clues that will help you determine the appropriate scope.

Technological Change

Many executives have been caught flat-footed by a new technology that deflated the scope of their enterprise almost overnight. Consider the sad fate of Iridium. The organization and its investors placed their bets on satellite technology that would permit worldwide phone calls and got blindsided by cellular technology. After launching their satellites, the company was unable to attract enough subscribers to pay interest on its start-up costs. The company went bankrupt and many were caught unaware that the best bet would have been to wait until the worldwide phone became smaller and cheaper.

Government Action, Regulation, and Laws

Is there legislation in place, pending, under consideration, or even anticipated that will affect your ability to alter your scope? For example, state legislators across the country are responding to their constituents' complaints about personal watercraft (such as the Jet Ski) by restricting their use. Needless to say, this will drastically affect the scope of the companies that manufacture them. That you familiarize yourself thoroughly with the potential repercussions of the regulatory climate as it pertains to your industry and that you do so prior to making any decisions on scope is vital and can't be overemphasized.

In sum, dealing effectively with scope requires that you examine and understand the issues that fall within these five key areas: economic, competitive, social, technological, and governmental. Unless you evaluate your scope options in the light of each factor, you are likely, as Oral Roberts did, to miss a decisive point.

Now let's discuss the three scope options individually: broadening scope, narrowing scope, and maintaining it as it is.

Broadening Scope

Tidel Engineering, the safe manufacturer we discussed earlier, represents a business that broadened its scope in an attempt to work its way out of a life-threatening crisis. With Tidel, it was either broaden or perish. Its excellent, high-quality safes had saturated its narrow market, and the company, which made no other product, urgently needed to expand its offerings. At this point, we will review the process that led to our solution, so you can observe the steps involved in enlarging scope.

The undeniable crisis had become so severe that most of Tidel's senior managers were looking for new jobs. We had no time to waste; we immediately brought together the entire organization, acknowledged that, indeed, the situation was do or die, and instructed everyone to make a list of everything that Tidel does well.

Unsurprisingly, making safes was the first answer. Next were so-called breadboards—the electronic boards containing the safes' mechanisms, alarms, timers, and so forth. But neither of these competencies was unique, and both were categorized as commodities. So we kept talking, thinking, and brainstorming.

That Tidel wasn't interested in becoming a subcontractor—that is, a supplier of safes and breadboards—was clear. Its goal was to manufacture an end product as it had the safes. Methodically, we worked through every possibility. The breadboards contained the technology needed to read swipe cards. How about an electronic food-stamp dispenser activated with a swipe card? No—the market was too limited. But the potential of the swipe card excited us. What else uses them? An ATM.

We researched ATMs and discovered that, at the time, no manufacturer sold one for less than $4,000, at which point it became obvious to everyone what Tidel's new direction would be.

By now, the whole process had taken about two weeks. Every day we worked in that room, had sandwiches brought in, and slowly made our way through Tidel's options. If we needed to conduct research, we did so. Every idea was thoroughly examined and debated. We appointed a devil's advocate who argued intelligently, attempting to deflate our ideas (a very useful strategy that we recommend).

We set a potential sales goal of $50 million; hence any idea with a more limited market was discarded. We knew from the beginning that Tidel needed to leverage its strengths—that is, its superb safes and electronic components. Over the months and years that followed, Tidel's management built on this idea, and today it is a leader in the ATM market. Leveraging is one of the key concepts in broadening scope.

If Tidel provides a working script for broadening scope during a crisis, the Walt Disney Company, which is the number two media conglomerate in the world (behind AOL Time Warner, Inc.), demonstrates how it can be done in less desperate circumstances. Although the organizations could scarcely be more different, they, like all companies involved in the process of changing scope, are subject to the fundamental principles that underlie it, such as the need to analyze every option in the contexts of all five external factors and the necessity of leveraging the strengths and competencies that will form the foundation of any augmented scope.

The late Walt Disney was an entertainment visionary. As he expanded the scope of his company, its success grew exponentially. Beginning humbly, producing short cartoons, the Walt Disney Company, which is based in Burbank, California, released its first animated feature, *Snow White and the Seven Dwarfs,* in 1937, after which Disney cannily recognized his capacity to leverage the popularity of his animated characters. Over time, he extended the organization into theme parks, live-action movies, and television shows. Almost as famous for his managerial style as for his creative brilliance, Disney built a strong corporate culture based on loyalty, high standards, and firm control. This culture proved perfect for an organization on a feverish growth tear that was fervently broadening its scope.

Following Disney's death, the company continued to augment its scope by acquiring a television network

(ABC), 7 theme parks, 27 hotels, 728 retail stores, 42 radio stations, 9 cable networks, 5 Internet sites, several Broadway theaters and touring theater companies, 2 sports teams (Anaheim Ducks and the Mighty Ducks of Anaheim), and 2 cruise ships. Though we don't know if Walt Disney himself would have embarked upon such a massive expansion, we do know that today, the company retains much of its original, unique culture—and certainly still leverages its animated characters.

Disney's successors have seen and seized many opportunities. Most consumers have a limited pool of disposable income and free time, which they allocate to a wide variety of leisure activities, such as books, movies, television, theater, sporting events, family outings, concerts, and fitness activities. Disney surveyed this landscape and realized that by broadening the scope of his entertainment offerings, he could capture a much bigger portion of the market. That his brand name, already one of the nation's most beloved, was known for consistently delivering high-quality, family-friendly products, made the decision to multiply the company's scope relatively easy. Unlike Tidel, Disney was operating from a position of strength.

It is worth repeating that these two very different organizations, which represent quite dissimilar challenges, share the same solution: Both broadened their scope.

Ramifications from Broadening Scope

Disney and Tidel are just two of many companies that have experienced a wide range of benefits from carefully orchestrated expansions of scope. But before focusing on the gains, let's clarify again that expansion requires a serious investment of resources and should not be undertaken without careful planning. Methodically exploring all possible scenarios, including worst-case ones, can minimize risk.

Having said that, we can move on to discuss the major advantages of broadening scope: making profits from new businesses; filling gaps in your product or service mix, thus strategically strengthening your existing businesses; thwarting competitors; creating consumer demands that fill production gaps during slack periods, enabling more efficient use of resources; and strengthening corporate identity, which enhances your organization's perceived value in the marketplace.

Let's look at these potential gains one at a time.

Making New Profit

Capturing new markets is the most compelling reason to broaden scope. Uno Restaurant Corporation, which operates the Pizzeria Uno pizza-restaurant chain and is based in West Roxbury, Massachusetts, began in Chicago, Illinois. It now offers prepared foods that are sold in grocery stores. In addition, it has added "carry-out—no-sit-down" pizza parlors. Because these ventures compete for segments of the dining-out market that aren't part of the original restaurants' domain, they don't cannibalize Pizzeria Uno's existing business.

Similarly, in 2001, the Ford Motor Company's Jaguar division introduced its X-type vehicle in a bold attempt to crack the under-$30,000 market, now dominated by Toyota Motor Corporation's Lexus and Bayerische Motoren Werke's BMW. The X-type has fewer cylinders than other Jaguars (six versus eight), is equipped with all-wheel drive, and is smaller overall than other Jaguars. This car's market niche doesn't overlap with existing Jaguar sales. If the scope expansion succeeds, it will strengthen Jaguar's brand name and generate new profits.

Keep in mind that the risk of each augmentation is that it may harm the reputation of the original business. Be aware, also, that profit opportunities may evaporate if unanticipated competition arises, if business operations prove troublesome, or if the expansion is motivated by the idea that "the grass is greener on the other side." Consider how quickly SyQuest Technology, Inc.'s breakthrough in large-capacity disk drives attracted competitors with equivalent or better products. And one competitor, Iomega Corporation, survived while SyQuest failed.

Though Woolworth Corporation's approach to changing scope differed from the methods employed by Uno Restaurant, it was, nonetheless, involved in the same process. While remaining a retail store, Woolworth switched its offerings completely after abandoning its original five-and-dime business in order to sell athletic footwear and apparel. But the company continued to struggle; it was a poor competitor in the shoe market and, in 1998, closed 570 shoe outlets. It also changed its name to the Venator Group, Inc. Careful planning and analysis can minimize such reverses, but the hazards of expanding remain if every aspect is not thoroughly considered.

Filling Gaps

Scope expansions designed to provide entry into a previously inaccessible market can pay off handsomely. For example, a grocery store that adds a liquor department may profit from an increase in grocery sales as well as from the alcohol sales.

Bertelsmann AG, the world's largest book publisher—its brands include Bantam, Ballantine, Doubleday, Knopf, and Random House—was concerned that Internet bookseller Amazon.com, Inc., could pose a threat. Envisioning a future in which Internet sales would account for a major share of book sales, where Amazon's clout would enable it to dictate terms and pricing unfavorable to other publishers, Bertelsmann expanded its scope by acquiring a 40 percent stake in Barnes & Noble, Inc.'s Internet entry, Barnesandnoble.com, Inc. In so doing, Bertelsmann is contesting Amazon.com's dominance.

The balance between cautiousness and boldness is tricky in the area of filling gaps. The Coca-Cola Company's addition of Dasani, a line of bottled water, to its other sugar-laden products fills a void with a large market following. Coming late to market as this product addition does, with well-established competitors in the field such as Poland Springs Water and Dannon Natural Spring Water, the Coca-Cola Company has to wage an uphill battle.

If executed confidently, filling gaps can yield nonfinancial as well as financial benefits. For example, Dell Computer Corporation added servers to its product line and, in so doing, established itself as a major computer vendor for corporations. Whether the servers were profitable wasn't the point—the expansion benefited Dell.

In fact, it is sometimes necessary to make unprofitable scope investments in order to enhance an organization's profits overall. For example, since certain major corporations will purchase only from suppliers who offer full product or service lines, some vendors are finding it necessary to carry money-losing add-ons.

Thwarting Competitors

Scope expansions that restrict competitors can make strategic sense. The Kellogg Company earns most of its profits from well-established cereal brands such as Frosted Flakes. When consumer demand for healthier breakfast alternatives reached a significant level, Kellogg introduced its own granola products. Even though these cereals aren't as profitable as Kellogg's staples, the expansion secured shelf space that might have been taken by a competitor.

Improving Resource Utilization

A carefully crafted scope expansion may generate new business during slack periods, thereby improving utilization rates for equipment and other resources. For example, the owner of a baseball stadium who confines its scope only to presenting baseball games will never get the stadium's utilization rate above, say, 40 percent. In contrast, the owner who leases the facility to concert promoters or other sports teams during the off-season, increases the utilization rate, which, in turn, boosts profits. An additional advantage is that the off-season customers become familiar with the facility, learn how to get there, and may return during the baseball season.

Scope expansions allow managers to distribute overhead expenses among multiple businesses, which translates into reduced unit costs for all products. United Parcel Service of America, Inc. (UPS) delivers packages Monday through Friday, but on Friday nights it also installs seats on some of its planes, which then fly charter passengers over the weekend.

Strengthening Corporate Identity

Finally, scope expansions create new business opportunities by burnishing and bolstering the corporation's identity, a strategy that has become commonplace in recent years. Just a few examples are Polo Ralph Lauren Corporation's decision to sell expensive house paints; Swiss Army Brands, Inc.'s foray into the watch business; and Martha Stewart Living Omnimedia, Inc.'s expansion into, well, just about everything. Honda Corporation proved to be resourceful and opportunistic when it used its outstanding reputation for quality automotive products to enter the lawn mower market, where it immediately achieved a sizable market share. In a similar vein, Harley-Davidson, Inc., a company whose motorcycles enjoy fervent devotion, now sells clothing in shopping malls.

Of course, a company that introduces an inferior product may tarnish, rather than polish, the luster of its entire franchise. Apple Computer, Inc., did just that when its first-generation personal digital assistant, the Newton, disappointed consumers. Despite the fact that the second-generation product was a good one, Apple could not reverse the earlier impression, which hurt the organization's attempt to introduce the second generation.

Expansions don't have to rely on the parent corporation's brand name, especially when the newer company's products fall outside the original organization's price point spectrum. In such cases, the parent's financial, logistical, organizational, and creative resources can remain invisible. The clothing lines spawned by Liz Claiborne, Inc.'s original products exemplify this approach. Targeting working women, the first line is midpriced and offers casual work clothes and accessories. The newer Dana Buchman line caters to executive women and is priced two or three times higher, and the Russ brand, which is priced 75 percent below Liz Claiborne, is aimed at cost-conscious women.

Although changing scope requires your complete attention, it need not—in fact, should not—be a protracted or complicated process. It entails getting inside an organization, studying its strengths and weaknesses, and then deciding if it should grow, shrink, or, in some cases, stay the same.

Advice that we give routinely to anyone trying to sort through scope-related issues is this: Some aspect of the organization will stand out very quickly if you are looking in the right place through the proper lens. Clearly, we are not implying that anything but the most studied and conscientious job will suffice; you must scrutinize the company and conduct as many interviews as necessary to determine what is and is not reliable data. Remember, though, that it doesn't take a genius to spot a goat in a flock of sheep. Something should stand out very quickly as you look at those sheep.

Narrowing Scope

Some years ago, a shirt manufacturer in the Northeast was trying to be all things to all people, making far too many items that included pullovers, men's dress shirts, and button-downs, all in every conceivable color. Furthermore, it was operating in three distinct markets, losing money in every one: private labeling, manufacturing for department stores, and supplying the mass-market, super-discount retailers. Our first conversation with its leaders went something like this.

"Are you the world's lowest-price producer of shirts?"

"Not at all."

"Then you don't belong in the super-giant-discount retail market. . . . What's your manufacturing time?"

"Usually 8 to 12 weeks because we have inefficiency problems. We manufacture in Ohio though we have plants down the East Coast."

"Okay, that eliminates private labeling because its required turnaround is a lot shorter and margins can be thinner. You can produce high quality, but you need a decent margin. That leaves one market to focus on— department stores—which will enable you to produce high-quality products but also capture a decent margin."

And it did. In this case, reducing scope was the right move, illustrating that paying attention to the interconnectedness of marketing demands and manufacturing capabilities can reveal a way to change scope.

Ways of narrowing scope are plentiful, and companies will find varying methods appropriate at different times for myriad reasons. Under the leadership of its founder, George Hatsopoulos, Thermo Electron Corporation, which is based in Waltham, Massachusetts, took a unique approach to reducing its scope. Like a corporate mother hen, Thermo acted as an incubator, nurturing companies as they developed around its technology. When they became viable, stand-alone entities, Hatsopoulos spun them off, selling a stake in each to the public. Following this model, Thermo sold off portions of what became 23 publicly traded companies.

Alternatively, the spun-out companies could have remained operating divisions within the parent corporation. That tactic would have expanded Thermo's scope, but it would also have required a complex bureaucratic structure to manage a mélange of diverse businesses. For Hatsopoulos, that option wasn't worth its price.

In March 1999, Thermo Electron reported negative results, and Richard F. Syron, the new chief executive officer, announced that the company would reduce, but not abandon, its reliance on the incubator strategy; and it bought back the outstanding shares of 12 of the 23 organizations that had been sold to the public. In January 2000, with static equity prices, Thermo Electron opted, again, to taper its scope by selling or spinning off noncritical businesses. Syron announced an aggressive plan to dramatically simplify Thermo Electron by focusing on "our core instrument businesses."

Perhaps the most important conclusion we can draw from Thermo Electron's constant tinkering is how easy it is to manipulate scope. Some organizations ruminate for years over a scope change, while Thermo adjusts it regularly, expanding or contracting it to fit the company's changing circumstances.

Reasons to Limit Scope

Here's an old adage: When you find yourself in a hole, the first thing to do is stop digging. This is really good advice when it comes to questions of scope. Suppose your business is laboring but failing to meet industry-standard profit margins. Don't explode. Take a deep breath and quell the urge to round up the usual suspects.

In trying times, businesspeople frequently feel compelled to make dramatic gestures, announce grand initiatives, or seek new opportunities and challenges when quite the opposite is often the better course. Some companies show sound judgment in stoutly resisting expanding their scope. Indeed, limited-scope policies have been the salvation of many organizations. We have identified four situations when this is the case.

1. *Insufficient resources—too little capital, too few smart managers and skilled workers, or a lack of some other resource necessary for success in a particular business.* Without adequate capital, most of the problems associated with scope expansion cannot be solved. Moreover, unanticipated events, such as the failure of predicted synergies—operational efficiencies resulting when companies with a common owner share resources—can precipitate capital shortages in the middle of a scope expansion. Such synergies should never be depended on to avert capital shortfalls. If a scope expansion is to have any chance of success, it must be adequately funded from the outset.

   Oakley, Inc., in Foothill Ranch, California, experienced the consequences of expanding scope without adequate capital. After winning the market for sunglasses, the company moved into athletic shoes in 1998. With its good instincts about Generation X and its considerable marketing talents, the logic of the expansion appeared sound. However, this was a market bristling with well-financed, entrenched companies, including New Balance Athletic Shoe, Inc.; Nike, Inc.; and Reebok International, Ltd. We attribute Oakley's misfortune here to its limited capital relative to its larger, already-established competitors. Oakley has changed strategies and now seeks a foothold in the sandals, hiking boots, and active urban footwear markets.

After capital, the second most powerful reason to apply the brakes to scope is a dearth of good managers and employees. Without them, expansion stumbles and organizations flounder. If you wonder why a successful and special restaurant in your hometown isn't franchised, the answer may be a shortage of necessary employees; its chefs, bartenders, wait staff, and managers cannot be cloned.

In the technological and professional fields, a paucity of employees impedes many expansions. The Mayo Clinic, considered one of the world's greatest medical centers, has cautiously expanded its scope beyond its original center in Rochester, Minnesota, and now has facilities in nearby Wisconsin and Iowa, as well as in Arizona and Florida. In contrast, some medical establishments expanded more aggressively and, in several cases, had to cut back later. In part, Mayo's caution reflects its concern that it would be unable to duplicate the marvelous staff of doctors, nurses, and technicians at its existing facilities.

Major League Baseball has not yet concluded that expanding its market scope into towns that don't adequately support the local franchise may be an error. Worse yet, this ambitious expansion dilutes the talent pool, harming the entire business because inferior players are needed to fill out the rosters. Many observers recommend that the league buy back the failing teams and use the better players in the remaining cities. Otherwise, the entire sport may be harmed.

The unavailability of other sorts of resources also present obstacles to enlarging scope. For example, if a pretzel company decides to brew beer using mountain-fed spring water in order to compete with Adolph Coors Company, it must locate its brewery near the water source, but that kind of real estate is hard to find.

An enterprise's reputation is a resource that must be preserved at all cost. If, say, an entertainment company wants to create a new record label, it must be able to withstand the early phases when its product list is preliminary and only unknown artists will sign with it. That is, the company's reputation must be exceedingly favorable so that neither its brand nor any other facet of the business is harmed by the developing record label. If it is not, the plans to broaden the scope in that direction should be put aside. Of course, it has to have adequate capital as well.

Consider the airline industry, where a shortage of airport landing gates (the resource, in this case) frequently prevents airlines from adding new flight routes. In cities with no additional gates, fares are high, because there is, literally, no room for new competitors; they are effectively barred from initiating service. But where landing gates are available, the fares drop to dissuade new competitors from flying that route.

2. *Insufficient experience in other businesses.* Lacking knowledge about another industry keeps many companies from expanding their scope. Many investment banks gave competitors a head start by not jumping on the Internet stock-trading bandwagon at the inception of Internet trading. In contrast, consider a telecommunication company's initial foray into cable television. After several months and millions of dollars, the company abandoned its plan to move cable over existing telephone lines when it realized it was not currently technologically feasible to do so.

3. *Sufficient success in a geographically limited market.* A desire to maintain geographic continuity prevents some organizations from broadening their scope. In a global economy, this may seem oddly antiquated, but it has distinct advantages: It allows managers to exert direct control; it minimizes confusion about zoning, regulatory, and cultural issues; and it fosters centralized relationships with banks, law firms, and accountants.

Many fine companies have chosen to remain within comfortable geographic boundaries: Drury Inn, Inc., a family-owned hotel chain, carefully selects which markets to enter so that it will avoid competing with the major chains. The Premor Refining Group, Inc., formerly Clark Refining Holdings, Inc., sells gasoline only in the Midwest. It is hard to argue with a scope-limiting strategy that yields a high return on investment, creates loyal customers and employees, and allows management to stay on top of the business.

4. *Insufficient management commitment.* Finally, many companies limit their scope because their managers are reluctant to assume complex management responsibilities that they don't fully understand. The exception that proves the rule is Sir Richard Branson, an exceptionally astute founder, chairman, and president of Virgin Group, Ltd. He has built an empire that includes airlines (Virgin Atlantic), beverages (Virgin Cola), a record label (Virgin), computer games, and lottery sales. How he develops, manages, and controls such a potpourri of businesses is rarely replicated. For the rest of us, clarity is sometimes found in simplicity.

How to Narrow Scope

As Thermo Electron has so convincingly demonstrated, if an organization has second thoughts about an expansion, it can reverse it by selling or liquidating unwanted assets. Several issues need to be explored when undertaking such actions; we will cover three. First, consider the timing of your plan; it can be important. Second, anticipate and manage your customers' reactions as well as those of the wider public. Third, prepare an accurate picture of the possible financial consequences.

On the issue of timing, it is never good to rush the sale; the buyer may sense your panic and exploit it by reducing what he or she will pay. On the other hand, an expedited sale frees managers' time and energy as well as other corporate resources that were tied up in the sale. While a profitable, growing division fetches a higher price than a distressed one, it is nonetheless a tactical mistake to delay the sale of the latter until it turns the corner. The cost of bringing the troubled unit up to par will most likely exceed the gains of doing so. Remember that a sale is preferable to a shutdown or liquidation (even when the seller is financing or subsidizing the purchaser) if the surviving businesses have the same customers as the closing operation.

Different algorithms determine how to implement scope reductions. The methods will vary depending on whether the unit to be jettisoned is part of the company's core business or is tangential to it. Dropping a unit that is not core will have fewer ramifications for the rest of the company but may affect the organization's image. Of primary importance to reducing scope at the core is being prepared for and managing consumers' perceptions so that remaining operations do not suffer.

Shedding a core business can be compared to a retail company's spring sale intended to get rid of surplus winter parkas. It is crucial that the retail store consider how customers will perceive such a sale: Will they expect similar sales in the future? Likewise, a company shedding a core business must ask: Will people perceive what remains of the organization and its products as inferior or damaged after the scope reduction? Of course, in a crisis or even in some turnaround situations, there may be little or no choice, and a core unit must be sold regardless of how customers will perceive it.

Although the overall objectives of restricting scope are to refocus the organization, reduce costs, retain current customers, and attract new ones, the critical activity is refocusing. Whatever is left of the company must be reassembled into an effective unit.

Maintaining Scope

Steinway & Sons started making and selling pianos in the United States in 1853. For a century and a half, the company's focus has remained resolutely fixed on pianos, and its instruments are acknowledged as among the world's best. And Steinway has not been complacent about its business. It pioneered revolutionary production methods while always insisting on the finest materials and instilling an enviable esprit de corps among its employees. The plan worked. Today the majority of piano concerts in the world are performed on Steinway & Sons instruments. In May 1995, Selmer, Inc., a maker of other musical instruments, bought the company and changed its name to Steinway Musical Instruments, Inc.

Did Waltham, Massachusetts–based Steinway forgo opportunities by focusing exclusively on pianos? It might have exploited its brand name to sell organs, trombones, handcrafted home furniture, even T-shirts imprinted with its logo. Yet it chose not to. It was a scope decision that answered the quintessential business question, "What is our mission?" Other companies' answers include maximizing profits, sales, or market share; producing a quality product; or protecting the workforce. Steinway's response was to develop a world-class reputation by doing one thing as perfectly as is humanly possible.

Don't Change Scope by Default

We will end this chapter with a little test.

Circle which of the following options we prefer.

- Broadening scope.

- Narrowing scope.

- Maintaining scope.

The correct answer is: None of the above. In fact, if you circled any of the phrases, sorry—you have failed the test.

In our view, getting bigger isn't necessarily getting better. Neither is getting smaller nor remaining static. None has intrinsic virtue; the context will determine the value.

Among your most important business decisions is what scope is best for your organization. Once you settle that, execute that decision and do so quickly. Don't let your present scope determine the size of your organization in the future, and above all else, never allow scope to shift by default, as if growing bigger, smaller, or not changing happens irrespective of your judgment. Doing so is irresponsible. Scope is to your company's financial status what your heart is to your health. Keep it going at the right pace, and you will thrive.

CHAPTER 3

Orient the Business

For all companies, old or new, launching a product that fails is inevitable and perhaps even a rite of passage. But when it happens more than once, you may be headed toward an abyss. Stop, think, and sweat out a remedy for turning your products into surefire hits.

Why do products fail? The primary reason is that the sellers aim them at the wrong buyers. If I want a Ford and you keep trying to sell me a Jaguar, you will soon be liquidating Jaguars. *Moral:* The road to wealth is paved with products that people actually need, dearly want, and will happily pay for. To get yourself on that road, aim your products at the right customers—those whose needs you fully understand and can truly satisfy.

One word describes this rifle-shot strategy: orientation. It derives from the Latin phrase for the act of looking eastward toward the Orient as the sun rises, which signifies birth. In our context, the birth is that of a great product oriented toward the precise market that awaits it.

Later in this chapter, we will look closely at specifically what a successful orientation involves, but for now, let's briefly consider why so many organizations repeatedly fail to orient their products toward their appropriate markets.

Time and again, executives and managers think they can ride ahead of the herd. Giddy with success, they think they have become instant geniuses. Let's skip all this market research, they say. Let's roll out this dandy new product right now and watch sales soar. They move in familiar cycles from success to arrogance or in reverse from failure to timidity, and they do so amidst confusion and miscalculations about what actual customers need and want. Even the best-managed and luckiest businesses may sometimes fail to recognize important shifts in market trends.

This happens when executives and managers make business decisions based more on their experience than on market data and research. Though understandable, this can be fatal, especially when the people working on a new product neither use it nor understand its intended audience.

Suppose you want to sell air-cooling devices to people whose incomes are less than $18,000. Your experience of a centrally air-conditioned country club won't help you sell this product. But millions of $35.00 window fans are sold every year in the United States, and the market in the underdeveloped world is vastly larger.

The worst thing you can do if you have missed a trend or misread a market is to deny that you have a problem. That will only compound the dilemma by preventing you from reacting intelligently, checking your orientation to make sure it is where you think it is, and rebounding quickly. In a volatile market, victory belongs to nimble organizations that spot the subtlest change and quickly fine-tune their orientation in response to it.

Discovering You Have an Orientation Problem

All sorts of things can weaken a company, from inept leadership to wobbly infrastructure, but the cruelest cut, which is also the most avoidable, is when your products aren't aligned with the market. How do you know when orientation is your primary problem and the one you *must* solve before you can address any others?

We have a fast, simple, effective answer: Listen to your frontline salespeople who deal with customers every day. They are your fingers on the pulse of the buyer and can tell you right away that, say, Kmart Corporation would take a million of your window fans if you incorporated two-tone styling, an automatic on-off timer, and cost no more than 20 percent above standard models. Kmart knows these fans will sell because it listens to its store managers, buyers, and sales associates.

Your salespeople have told you straight on, with unimpeachable authority, that you must adjust your orientation. Distinguishing your product so that it appeals to customers who have numerous choices of low-cost fans, all of which move air equally well, is imperative.

Every day, salespeople have the experience of walking in to pitch a product to some national chain and finding three other salespeople from competing companies waiting to do the same. Each of you has a product that fills a need for the market that you are targeting. When it is your turn, the chief buyer tells you that she still has a product she bought from you a year ago that sat on the shelf for eight months, and she still can't get rid of it. Worse, one of your competitors has a product that is of poorer quality, but it is selling like hotcakes: Its price is what is moving it. Or she may tell you that you are at the right price point, but your product has a notorious reputation for breaking on its way out the door, and she is taking back 12 percent of everything you have shipped in the last nine months. Clearly, you have a quality problem. And how likely is your product to win a healthy share of the market if it breaks so quickly?

Rely on your salespeople to be your early-warning system. If you are disoriented in the market at a particular price point or standard of quality, they will be the first to know.

Now, let's look at a real example of an orientation that didn't work, primarily because market trends were favoring larger competitors. In this case, although the beleaguered organization failed to reposition itself and went under, a new company bought its properties and oriented it successfully. Both enterprises provide valuable lessons on orientation.

Sun TV & Appliance, Inc., operated a chain of stores in and around Columbus, Ohio. From the perspective of price, the retail chain was well positioned until it collided with the buying power of giants such as Best Buy Co., Inc., and Circuit City Stores, Inc., at which point it was selling the same products as they at higher prices. Needless to say, its orientation was unenviable. When we were hired to rescue Sun, we realized immediately that, unlike its competitors, it could not afford to build a new state-of-the-art distribution center to reduce delivery costs. Next, we shut down Sun's outlying stores to, in effect, draw the wagons into a tighter circle to make distribution more cost efficient.

In the end, that wasn't enough. We had to sell the vast majority of stores to a corporation outside Sun's orientation, H.H. Gregg Appliances & Electronics Company, which threw out all the radios and CD players and converted the stores to sell washing machines, dryers, and television sets. The market perception was totally different: The new owner was no longer competing in the general electronics business.

Sun TV did very well until the big players moved in and undercut its prices. Had we sold at their prices, we would have made 1 percent over our cost, demonstrating the power of quantity buying and a huge advertising budget. In addition, Best Buy and Circuit City had almost unlimited advertising budgets.

How Orientation Works

Orientation, as we see it, isn't a fixed and immutable condition; it is an ongoing process in which adjustments are made to accommodate changes in customers' needs, desires, expectations, and perceptions. Since all orientations, whether brilliantly or poorly designed, share certain aspects, we will examine some general principles to get a clearer picture of why some efforts at market positioning succeed and others fail.

In orientation, as in all aspects of business, the customer has the last word. Theories of consumer behavior are worthless if they don't explain why customers buy or don't buy. Orientation, itself, is meaningless if it doesn't align the product with the customer. There is a saying down in Texas: "Just because a chicken has wings doesn't mean it can fly." Just because you have conceived a brilliant market orientation scheme doesn't mean that people are rushing to buy your products.

Generally speaking, orientation describes how a company presents itself to the marketplace and how customers perceive its products or services. In our view, orientation has two parts: value and utility. When a company positions its product or service in relation to those of its competitors, it is setting the value and utility of that item. Adopting the wrong orientation—that is, setting value and utility levels that don't work for the market—harms even the best products or services. Conversely, the right orientation can make successes out of so-so offerings.

The most important value decisions are what kind of product or service to offer and what to charge for it. The most important utility decision is which individuals and groups you should target as potential customers.

Neither value nor utility is an absolute in our orientation model; each is on a continuum ranging from high to low.

High value means that the customer regards your product or service as a good buy (sometimes, despite a high price tag) based on its quality. Ford Motor Company founder Henry Ford was a master of creating an impression of high value. "The public should always be wondering," he once said, "how it is possible [for this company] to give so much for the money."

High utility means that attributes other than perceived value, such as availability and ease of use, make a product or service appealing to a wide variety of customers.

Table 3.1 summarizes the four orientation strategies that result from value and utility combinations. Remember that we are dealing with continuums so each box actually covers a range of orientations.

TABLE **3.1** Orientations and the Value/Utility Trade-off

	High Value	Low Value
High Utility	**High/High** The Prestige Orientation	**High/Low** The Utility Orientation
Low Utility	**Low/High** The Value Orientation	**Low/Low** The Contemptuous Orientation

A combination of high value and high utility (top-left box) produces what we call the prestige orientation. Examples include Mercedes automobiles or Rolex watches, items for which certain consumers will pay top dollar for what they perceive as top quality.

The top-right box places utility relatively higher than value, creating the utility orientation. Fast-food restaurants that provide high utility by their omnipresence, low cost, and fast service are examples. They are low value to the customer who prefers better food in more pleasant surroundings.

When value is ranked higher than utility, as in the bottom-left box, the value orientation is created. Traditional army-navy surplus stores reflect a value orientation by selling items with limited appeal (such as camouflage suits); they find buyers because their merchandise appears to be a good value and can't be found anywhere else.

We call the bottom-right box the contemptuous orientation, because it combines low value and low utility in ways that show disrespect for the customer. Regulated enterprises tend to fall in this category. Though limited funds or political constraints may account for some of the problems, they can't explain why such organizations often behave as though the customer is at fault, which must be the worst mistake any enterprise can make in the area of orientation. We would argue that a good example of a contemptuous orientation is one characterized by poor service, high prices, and little opportunity to meet customer demands. The quality of its service is poor, including trains that are old, schedules that aren't adhered to, stations that are about to collapse, and prices that are high.

Let's flesh out these abstractions by looking briefly at two companies that occupy different positions along the value and utility continuums of our orientation model.

Laura Ashley Holdings PLC

The Laura Ashley clothing chain boasts a prestige orientation that gives it an up-market aura throughout the United Kingdom. It sells an expensive line of clothes and home furnishings, including casual apparel and linens. Giving little thought to how the U.K. and U.S. markets differ, Laura Ashley shipped its orientation across the Atlantic Ocean and opened shops in a string of malls that were designed to look like their very proper English cousins. Initially, Laura Ashley achieved some success with its high-end flowery designs and bright colors. But the appeal of English tradition wasn't strong enough to attract bargain-hunting, novelty-seeking mall shoppers in the United States. The Brits were virtually malled to death. With the wrong orientation, Laura Ashley watched its sales tumble and eventually closed or downsized many of its U.S. outlets.

Marriott International, Inc.

"Different strokes for different folks" seems to describe Marriott International's orientation strategy. While its competitors offer homogenous units (identical room design, lobby, and bar of soap for every guest in every hotel), Marriott has moved in the opposite direction by offering seven distinct "brands" of hotels, each of which targets a different market segment. It has a hotel for every budget. Ritz-Carlton is at the high end with rooms costing $400 or more per night; Residence Inns are in the middle range with rooms for about $100 a night; and Fairfield Inns are at the bottom with rooms starting at $49 per night. Given all this variety, it appears that a huge majority of U.S. travelers will lay their heads on Marriott pillows this night and every other in the foreseeable future. Indeed, Marriott contends for customers at every price point of this country's 1 billion hotel rooms. When Marriott increases its rates, it simultaneously provides more amenities at every level. Ritz-Carlton, for instance, offers butler service, while Fairfield Inns offer free 24-hour self-serve coffee and tea. Both apparently deliver exactly what their consumers want.

All of these Marriott chains are profitable. With precision, the company pinpointed every brand's orientation and made sure that the combinations of value and utility appealed to the targeted market segment. Furthermore, Marriott has succeeded in showing the public that its multitiered service isn't a sign of confusion, but a clear boon to travelers. It offers a room with the amenities you want at a price you care to spend.

Taken together, these snapshots of two companies reveal some hard truths about orientation. First, if many consumers are fickle and hard to please, they also have long memories. Thus, while it may be extremely difficult to sustain a successful orientation, wrong ones are just as difficult to excise from the minds of the buying public.

Yet despite its being tentative or even misrepresenting the enterprise, a company's orientation defines where it wants to go. Choosing a prestige, value, or utility strategy sets a course for the whole organization. Then, specific tactics, which we will look at later in this chapter, move the organization toward its goal.

Once the consumer places your products within one of the four orientation categories (prestige, utility, value, contemptuous), it will be very hard to change his or her mind, and trying to do so will be expensive. In some cases, the perception of a brand is so fixed that you have to develop an alternate brand to create a new perception.

Suppose, for example, that Kmart wanted to convert from an everyday-low-price orientation to an upscale retailer. First, it would have to confront the fact that customers tolerate its sometimes minimal service because they are eager to save money. So, before it tampers with its price positioning, Kmart would have to consider how to improve service. Overcoming a market's perception about your product is almost always an enormous, complex undertaking, and you must prepare for a long haul.

The worst perception to encounter is that your goods are poor quality, expensive, but not necessary.

The Keys to a Successful Orientation

Implementing an orientation strategy successfully usually involves tactical decisions and appropriate action in five critical areas. In three, your goal is to establish value; in the other two, it is to create utility (see Figure 3.1). Some products or services may not involve all five areas.

Value

An item's price, quality, and durability define its value. Consumers create a composite metric of value in which they trade higher prices against superior quality or durability. The metric summarizes consumers' overall assessments, which are reflected in comments such as, "it's a good buy" or "it isn't worth the money." Interestingly, corporate managers who adjust the three factors (price, quality, and durability) to determine the desired value target never know exactly what weight customers give to each factor.

For most products or services, value depends on all three factors, though for some, such as commodities, only one or two are relevant. For example, since units of gold or units of wheat are identical, only price matters. If items are consumed at the time of purchase, such as popcorn at the movies, value depends on price and quality; durability is irrelevant. Quality and durability, but not price, establish the relative value of items purchased for long-term personal care, such as wheelchairs or exercise equipment.

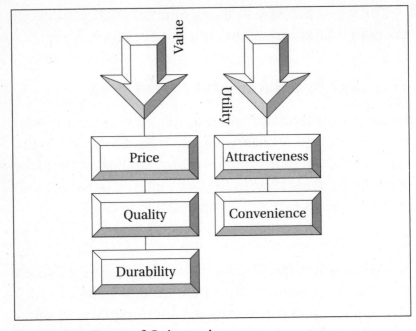

FIGURE 3.1 Parts of Orientation

In some situations a single characteristic dominates the value metric. Only price matters when the consumer's goal is to impress others. Would Volkswagen AG's Rolls-Royce Motor Cars sell as many vehicles at a lower price? At the opposite extreme, decisions to purchase Societe BIC's BIC pens (more than 20 million sold every day) are based on their low price.

Mountain climbers insist on durability since their lives depend on reliable equipment. In contrast, the fact that durability can be ignored is the central selling point for disposable cameras, disposable syringes, and disposable eating utensils.

When people buy medicines, they are influenced solely by the products' quality. One doesn't choose a heart medicine by comparing prices, unless two are identical.

The combination of its price, quality, and durability categorizes an item in a value grade somewhere between high and low. The objective is not always to create the highest value possible. If it were, paper clips would be solid gold. Rather, your goal is to use the three value factors to set a price that will appeal to a spectrum of your customers.

Companies that sell similar products or services mix the value components to attain the value metric appropriate for their particular customers. For example, although L.L. Bean, Inc., and Family Dollar Stores, Inc., sell fundamentally similar tents, L.L. Bean charges top prices for them, while Family Dollar Stores maintains its reputation for low prices. Bean's customers are satisfied because, in their view, they are buying a high-value item with superior quality, which carries a lifetime guarantee. Family Dollar's patrons are content, because they have received good value for their money.

Often the advertising for a product or service indicates where the organization that makes it wants it to fit in the value metric. Examples are easy to find. For quality: "The power to be your best" (Apple Computer, Inc.); "Doesn't your dog deserve Alpo" (Nestle, S.A.'s pet food). For durability: "Even a policeman can get stuck in traffic" (Tag-It Pacific, Inc.'s Talon zippers); "It's everywhere you want to be" (Visa International, Inc.). For price: "Always Low Prices" (Wal-Mart Stores, Inc.).

Utility

If value relies on price, quality, and durability; utility, represented in Figure 3.2, considers convenience and attractiveness. Like value, utility is part and parcel of orientation.

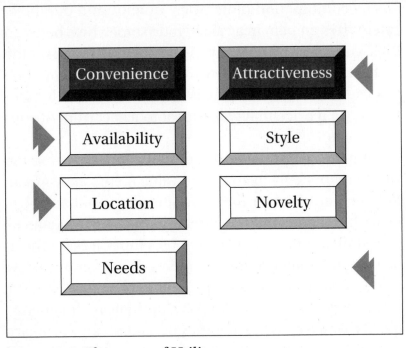

FIGURE 3.2 Elements of Utility

Convenience means that an item is available when a customer wants it; it is easy to buy and use, and it is sold by a merchant who is sensitive to customer needs and worries. Utility is enhanced by convenience, but adding it is usually expensive. In order to increase availability, for instance, a company may have to invest in new inventories or computer servers (for virtual businesses); develop sites in new locations; and fund training and hiring programs to heighten employees' awareness of customers' needs.

Attractiveness, the primary components of which are style and novelty, also contributes to utility. Because attractiveness is subjective, people's views on style and novelty in a product or service will differ. Nevertheless, a company's decisions in this area can make or break that product or service. The choices of style can be broadly categorized as classic, bland, and avant-garde. Classic styling is widely accepted; bland is nondescript or utilitarian; and avant-garde styling is cutting edge. About novelty, which is at least as subjective as style, the only thing that people agree upon is that the wrong amount of it will alienate customers.

The items that consumers consider more attractive will rank higher in utility. Good managers spot them quickly, or else sales suffer.

Customers' preferences in utility can be calculated on a metric similar to the one used to determine value, but this metric reflects perceptions toward an item's convenience and attractiveness. The importance given to either factor will vary to the extent that people's tastes and their views of the product do. Still, a product that is both convenient and attractive is certain to yield more utility than one that is not. For an example, Table 3.2 outlines the utility factors found in various ways of clothes shopping.

At Gianni Versace, SpA, the exclusive Milan, Italy–based fashion house, a personal shopping assistant (demonstrating high attention to customer needs) works with the customer; in addition, its merchandise carries a specific cachet. Versace is a high-utility merchant.

The J. Crew Group, Inc.'s J. Crew catalog is a medium-utility merchant. On one hand, it sells stylish and trendy goods that shoppers love. On the other hand, some con-

TABLE 3.2 Utility from Clothing Shopping

	High Convenience	Low Convenience
High Attractiveness	**High/High** Versace High utility	**High/Low** J. Crew Catalogue Medium utility
Low Attractiveness	**Low/High** Having mom buy it Medium utility	**Low/Low** Sears Low utility

sumers dislike shopping by phone: selection is based on photographs, delivery takes a few days, and returns require a trip to the post office. Finally, the most convenient shopping technique is when someone else does it for you: no hassles, no lines, and no painful decisions.

On rare occasions a bandwagon effect may rattle customers' already established assessments of utility. A bandwagon occurs when everyone wants the same product at the same time. Hasbro, Inc.'s Furbies, one of 1999's most popular holiday presents, and Sony Corporation's PlayStation 2 in 2000 rode a bandwagon effect that emptied store shelves. The utility ranking of these products skyrocketed as the bandwagon inflated everyone's estimates of their attractiveness. The fact that convenience was reduced because the items were so hard to find was more than compensated for by the enormous boost to their attractiveness that resulted from the huge promotional effort. Shortages that enhance desire are beneficial to utility.

Setting Orientation

Managers choose a company's orientation when they set value and utility levels for products or for the entire company, which they do either deliberately, by selecting levels, or by default, when they respond defensively to a competitor's action. Needless to say, actively setting orientation is the better method. That way, managers can coordinate their decisions on several products, which maximizes the combined impact and minimizes the cost of those products. A passive orientation strategy, which means that someone else is declaring the position of your product or service, is dangerous. The analogous situation in warfare is allowing the opposing commander to determine when and where a battle will occur. Managers who dodge the responsibility of setting orientation may not understand the intricacies of their product or their customers. Or they may lack the confidence to define a new direction.

We view setting a price point as the most critical orientation decision. Low prices offer what economists call the elasticity effect, which stimulates sales. If a high price reduces sales, it can also improve net margins. Consider the substantial price difference between the $8 that Ameritrade, Inc., an Internet company, charges to buy or sell any amount of stock and the $300 that a mainline Wall Street firm charges to sell a relatively small amount of stock. These are two very different pricing strategies that both work.

Ideally, a business wants its sales and profits to grow rapidly, but often it must settle for one or the other. A common strategy is to charge low prices initially (or distribute coupons or other discounts) to attract business, then raise them later. The flaw here, though, is that the strategy risks misrepresenting the company's orientation, which may anger consumers when prices go up. The American Express Company is a case in point. It introduced free stock trading in order to attract new customers quickly but then instituted commissions, upsetting many of its new clients, some of whom returned to their old brokers. A more astute tactic is to charge a high price initially but include sufficient value and utility to offer a prestige orientation. American Express's mistake may have been to think only about prices and to ignore orientation.

A successful orientation is always temporary. Customers and their preferences change, technology advances, and new sources and forms of competition can quickly unhinge a useful orientation. Look, for example, at the changing fortunes of Miami Beach, which in the 1950s and 1960s was a desired vacation spot. Then, when places such as Hawaii and the Virgin Islands became more accessible because of better airline service, cheaper fares, and myriad package deals, more and more vacationers gravitated to those places. Hotels in Miami failed to respond to the new competition soon enough, and by the mid-1970s, Miami Beach had become a destination mainly for retirees. Without vacationers, the area declined. Its rebirth began as hoteliers, restaurateurs, and merchants became savvy about competing for vacation dollars, and by the early 1990s, helped by an art deco retro craze, Miami Beach was again a desirable vacation spot.

Is there any way to guarantee that your company's orientation will never slip? Unfortunately, that would take a degree of clairvoyance not available to ordinary mortals.

Predicting how consumers' tastes, competitors' actions, or technology will change is beyond the capacities of most managers. However, they should be alert and prepared to respond quickly and decisively to unexpected events.

In fact, managers' training should emphasize the importance of being patient and not switching orientations too quickly. If it is a mistake to recognize a faulty orientation too slowly, it is an equally egregious error to be too eager to change your market positioning. While changes in orientation are easy to formulate, they are brutally difficult to carry out successfully; thorough testing and evaluative procedures should precede all major decisions.

Managers may be tempted to employ the strategies that led to thriving companies the previous year. Instead, they should concentrate on finding the right niche for the future. Of course, we aren't recommending that you ignore new opportunities, only that you focus solely on those that are a good match for you. Companies should not be in constant motion trying one orientation, then jumping to the next; at the same time, they should know when it is time to relinquish one that isn't working.

Leaders of flourishing companies fine-tune their orientations constantly. And they transform their businesses as well as their products in the process of seeking a winning mix of value and utility for their markets. Troubled companies can achieve the Phoenix Effect by restructuring their orientation.

What are the consequences of changing your orientation too slowly or too quickly? Oklahoma Tire & Supply Company (OTASCO), once a huge retailer and now out of business, made both mistakes. OTASCO built its entire empire of more than two hundred stores in the Midwest on a simple promise: There, you could buy tires as well as all large household appliances—refrigerators, freezers, washers, dryers—on a reasonable monthly payment schedule.

As you may have guessed, this organization grew up in the 1930s and 1940s before everyone had at least one all-purpose credit card, such as a MasterCard or Visa. Inevitably, in the early 1980s, OTASCO floundered as people discovered that the discount stores offered more than lower prices; with their credit cards, shoppers could finance their purchases themselves. OTASCO deteriorated further as MasterCard and Visa gained popularity.

OTASCO tried to change its orientation by promoting low prices every day instead of monthly plans, but it didn't have the infrastructure to support moving additional low-priced units. Then, the company's marketing campaigns got too far ahead of its infrastructure.

OTASCO's managers arranged for some of its inventory to be drop-shipped directly from the manufacturers to the stores because the company's antiquated distribution centers could not respond quickly enough. The organization wasn't capable of informing the warehouse that a particular model was out of stock until someone noticed it and placed the order. And that was too long a delay for many customers. OTASCO wasn't set up to manage its supply chain with the most up-to-date method, which calls for always having at least one of every model of every unit in stock at most stores. Furthermore, within that system, the distribution center automatically shipped an additional unit to keep the store stocked with two. That OTASCO failed to build the infrastructure that such a system required, meant that if a manager forgot to order a particular unit, a customer who thought her order had been placed was about to be disappointed. Worse was when people came to the stores having just finished reading the company's Sunday newspaper ad circular to be told, "Sorry, we sold our last unit, and I don't have a clue when we'll have more in stock." Understandably, customers took their business elsewhere.

OTASCO exemplifies what could happen when a company tries to change its orientation without thinking through whether its infrastructure could support the change. It could not compete with stores that built their infrastructure first, then developed their marketing and sales strategy around it.

More recently, we have seen companies doing precisely the reverse; they are building their infrastructures before knowing the results of their marketing campaigns—that is, how many customers the marketing will attract. Many Internet grocery delivery operations used all of their initial public offering monies to build the warehouses and automated systems they assumed they would need to service the perceived onslaught of online grocery orders that their business models needed. But when they launched their Internet sites, they realized they had too few customers to support the infrastructure. Online grocery shopping and home delivery weren't quite ready for prime time. Orientation errors, high prices, and customers' reluctance to trust the quality of fruits, vegetables, and meats selected by someone else contributed to the demise.

In contrast, Blockbuster, Inc., seems to be moving toward a promising future orientation at exactly the right pace. Envisioning a future in which most people will download their movies online, Blockbuster is dipping into these uncharted waters one toe at a time.

Twenty years from now, Blockbuster may see itself out of the brick-and-mortar business. Still, it realizes that converting to an entirely online business poses formidable problems in that it has to reorient itself in relation to its customers. And people aren't yet ready to give up the ritual of picking up a movie on the way home from work. In other words, there may always be a niche for the brick-and-mortar video rental store.

Making assumptions about what consumers will and won't prefer is always risky, especially when you are considering adjusting your company's orientation. When cell phones first came out, companies mistakenly assumed that people would want to pay for their calls the same way they paid for home service—by accruing a bill that they paid at the end of the month. As it turned out, a whole segment of the population was concerned about running up large cell phone bills. That concern led to the implementation of the prepaid card. Most likely, the people who buy them are aware that they are paying a premium, but the assurance of knowing they can't exceed the card's credit limit makes it worth the higher price.

Changing Orientation

Asked to give just one piece of advice on maintaining a successful orientation, we would say: "Keep in touch with your customers." Nothing contributes more to your decision-making process than your customers' input.

Ignore your customers' needs and expectations, and you will get into trouble. If your orientation loses its moorings in the marketplace, you may need to completely over-haul it, which is an enormously difficult, very expensive, and time-consuming job. That most people have not yet been involved in an orientation change means they will probably require the help of outside consultants.

Given the risks, what are the conditions, if any, that would make changing orientation the most appropriate move for a company? We will approach this by looking at situations where reorientation isn't a good idea.

We never recommend a dramatic change in orientation for a business in the midst of a major turnaround or in crisis. In either situation, cash will be short, bankers' patience limited, and everyone will be distracted by the loud ticking of the clock.

Without the pressure of time, reorientation is a more attractive, though by no means the only reasonable, option. We are more likely to recommend reorientation when something specific has shifted in the company's competitive environment. For example, new government legislation prevents you from importing some of the low-cost goods that your business depends upon. Even then, we won't necessarily suggest introducing a new brand. Instead, we would probably advise the company to keep the old brand and, at the same time, develop a new one. That way, the same sales force can use its contacts for the new brand and reposition them both with different price points.

A situation much like this occurred a number of years ago when Sears, Roebuck & Company wanted to appeal to different markets and change its orientation simultaneously. One of its first steps was an advertising campaign that promised consumers their choice of good-, better-, or best-quality products. Actually, the company wanted its orientation to fall in the better and best categories, but it had many customers looking for good quality—say, a hammer for under $9—that it didn't want to lose. Sears campaigned heavily to develop market awareness of its stores' three levels of utility and value. It is an interesting example of using straightforward language to convey a rather complex orientation that promised almost everything to nearly everyone. As it turned out, the strategy may have worked less well than anticipated; the stores had to carry many additional products to cover all three quality levels, which led to higher inventories. Eventually, Sears dropped the middle category and worked with *good* and *best*. This concept has evolved into building separate brands for products of different quality.

Despite the expense and complexity of altering core products' orientations, we know that many companies will attempt it, either because they need to or because they hope to capture new markets as a result. That very few will succeed in their efforts is something we also know.

Based on that, we frequently recommend to chief executives that an acquisition may be the safest route to reorientation, not, however, because they are quick or easy. In fact, finding and negotiating a suitable acquisition can take two to three years. You have to allow time for the bankers to do their piece, and, in the case of international acquisitions, to determine other issues such as demand, cultural differences, and currency. What you are doing, in effect, is buying someone else's orientation—picking up real estate in a market niche you want to occupy, which can be much less costly and risky than new products that may or may not change your market orientation.

It may be that as time goes on, our views on orientation will be less useful as guidelines for action than as a context or perspective for reviewing your company and its business. Dealing, as it does, with the interface of your products and your customers, orientation brings to the surface the concerns that are most relevant to any organization that sells products or delivers services—aiming your product or service at the right audience is an example. We urge you to bring our concepts of "value metric" and "utility metric" into your staff meetings and take note of how they affect your associates' perceptions of both your products and your customers.

CHAPTER 4

Manage Scale

Best Buy Co., Inc., and Circuit City Stores, Inc., are in the same business: Both sell electronic equipment and accessories at retail. But they have made very different decisions about the scales of their stores. All of Best Buy's facilities are more or less the same size—approximately 44,000 square feet. In contrast, Circuit City constructs stores in four major sizes (about 9,000, 13,000, 15,000, and 23,000 square feet) and two smaller sizes for malls of approximately 2,000 and 3,000 square feet. With sales of about $12 billion in 2000, each company has prospered, but Best Buy's selling costs consistently consume a smaller percentage of its revenues, which translates into higher profit margins. The store size—that is—its increased scale, may give Best Buy the slight edge of economies of scale.

At one time, economies of scale were synonymous with megafactories and vast industrial complexes, but today they are viewed through a more encompassing lens. They include business considerations, such as the size of an advertising budget, the establishment of brand names, the capacity to fund ongoing maintenance, the distribution of costs over a wide spectrum of operations, and the versatility inherent in diverse locations.

Clear Channel Communications, Inc., is a multibillion-dollar advertising company of sorts that operates through its diversified media holdings. With the aim of achieving a scale that would attract major advertisers, it has sought omnipresence in every media arena by merging and acquiring companies. As a result of mergers with AMFM, Inc., and SFX Entertainment, Inc., Clear Channel has nearly 900 radio stations in the United States, another 240 overseas, 19 television stations, more than 500,000 display billboards, and 120 live entertainment venues. The concept behind this media octopus is that it becomes a one-stop shop for major marketers, such as the Procter & Gamble Company. Referring to the enhanced size, Robert F.X. Sillerman, whose SFX Corporation was acquired by Clear Channel for $4.4 billion in August 2000 and who remains SFX's executive chairman, pointed out that content and distribution will work to strengthen each other. By combining all forms of media, Clear Channel intends to siphon advertisers from other providers. It seeks scale economies that extend across each medium. Compared with other vendors, it will not provide a better cost advantage in, say, radio, but it will lower the total price of radio advertising.

As an operation grows, businesses typically, though not inevitably, achieve efficiencies that reduce the percentages that are subtracted from gross revenues for product development, manufacturing, distribution, and marketing. Moreover, the greater a company's scale advantage, the more it can protect its market share by effectively barring entry to its competitors. In the well-planned cases, increases in size provide a new pool of investment funds that allow you to take immediate advantage of where the market is moving. You can afford to pay a premium to buy a young, entrepreneurial competitor that has carved out a product segment in a corner of your market that you overlooked. Buying that upstart can put you right back into the game.

But economies of scale aren't innate to growth. They must be managed into existence with the utmost care. Not achieved through a formal initiative, they are developed as a shared value within an organization.

If we look at the colossal Wal-Mart Stores, Inc., we see that its economies of scale begin at its corporate home, which brings to mind a collection of mundane, unadorned buildings, add-ons, and warehouses. Through its quite ordinary collection of structures, Wal-Mart is sending a very clear message: "As big as we are and as much money as we make, our aim is not to impress ourselves or anyone else. Low cost is our focus, and we know how to squeeze a penny."

While Wal-Mart's strategy—to succeed as a low-cost producer—has guided its decisions about scale, its headquarter's operations have grown in response to its increasing business. Unlike some companies, it wasn't seduced by the potential advantages of scale into building an expensive corporate campus or living lavishly beyond its earnings in any other way. Like other successful chief executives, Wal-Mart's, beginning with founder Samuel Moore Walton, proceeded cautiously and gradually.

When planning for information technology needs, some chief executives insist on leasing instead of buying what they need. Doing so allows them to trade the equipment in later for larger, upgraded systems, which means they avoid being stuck with obsolete models. And leasing doesn't limit growth in any way. Another approach is to sign with a data management and storage company that offers arrangements that allow you to pay only for the storage that you actually use. If you need more capacity, it's possible to double, triple, or quadruple your allotment. Moreover, you can always move data storage equipment in-house later, if doing so becomes preferable.

The Quest for Larger Scale

Clearly, attaining larger scale has been a major preoccupation of businesses over the past 15 years. Corporations can set out to achieve it in two ways: (one) by merging with or acquiring other companies or, (two) by spurring their own growth.

The 1990s could well be called the era of mass mergers. Daimler Benz Aktiengesellschaft initiated a wave of consolidation that swept the automotive industry when Daimler Benz merged with Chrysler Corporation and created DaimlerChrysler AG. Next, the Ford Motor Company bought the automotive division of Volvo AB after first purchasing Jaguar PLC, following which Nissan Motor Company agreed to cooperate with Renault SA. Some industry experts predict that when the automakers finish amalgamating each other, fewer than six independent companies will remain standing. Grocery store chains, too, such as the Kroger Co., Safeway, Inc., and Albertson's, Inc., have gobbled up small local and regional chains, including the Skaggs Alpha Beta Company, the Star Market Company, and Fred Meyer, Inc. As acquisitions augment their scale, the giant stores have penetrated new territories or solidified their dominance in their established market areas.

Such consolidations represent just the tip of the iceberg. Banking, pharmaceuticals, airlines, hotels, and funeral homes are just some of the industries in which businesses have been combining for the primary purpose of economic efficiencies. The potential for reducing costs with this method varies across industries. In some cases, companies will experience substantial unit-cost savings as soon as production increases; others will see only modest cost changes. Businesses that buy more nonlabor inputs (machines, equipment, or real estate) generally gain the most from economies of scale, because machine productivity tends to grow exponentially, while machine costs rise geometrically. That is, increasing your spending by 20 percent will buy you a computer that is 100 percent faster or an airplane that holds 50 percent more seats.

Table 4.1 is a hypothetical model of the cost differences among three competitors in the same industry, each of which has a progressively smaller output. The most efficient organization, the giant company, pays, on average, per unit costs that amount to half of those paid by the smallest enterprise, and a third less than what the midsize company pays.

The giant company could match the prices its competitors charge, thereby earning a higher profit margin. Or it may decide to use its cost advantage to take market share away from competitors. In a value-oriented market (where decisions are based on price and quality), the low-cost

TABLE **4.1** Cost Differences among Three Unequally Sized Competitors

	Output	Average Cost per Unit
Giant company	450	$1.00
Medium company	300	$1.50
Smallest company	200	$2.00

company's prices might even eliminate the other organizations. The point is that regardless of the giant company's tactic, it is benefiting significantly from scale. Of course, a merger between the medium and small companies would create a very large competitor with output of 500 units, which could have an average unit cost of less than $1.

Yahoo! Inc. is a key Internet portal that has evolved into a global media company. Early on, Yahoo! focused almost exclusively on attaining scale, which it measured by counting the number of visitors to its site. Along with other Internet-spawned companies, its stock price soared in 1999 and into 2000, as investors bet on its future. A large part of the investors' optimism can be attributed directly to scale economies. From 30 million users at the end of 1998, the number of registered Yahoo! users rose to approximately 180 million at the end of 2000. Having reached that scale, its cost per user declined sufficiently for Yahoo! finally to become profitable. Revenues grew from $245 million in 1998 to $591 million in 1999, and $1.1 billion in 2000. And during the same period, net income reversed from a negative $13.6 million in 1998 to a positive $47.8 million in 1999, and $70.8 million in 2000. In response, Timothy Koogle, then Yahoo!'s president and chief executive officer, remarked, "We are really starting to see the law of big numbers" (Kara Swisher, "Yahoo's Quarter Net Tops Expectations," *Wall Street Journal*, October 8, 1998, p. B5). He was referring to economies of scale. The future may hold even bigger profits for Yahoo! if more users sign on every day.

That large scale is crucial becomes obvious when you consider the difficulty your business encounters if its rival's average cost is $1 per unit while yours is $1.50 or even $2 per unit.

Every discounter selling in the same market as Wal-Mart confronts that organization's 5 to 10 percent higher gross margin—the result of its lower average cost. Wal-Mart has decimated its competition with this advantage: The landscape is littered with the wreckage of small discounters.

Combining several small-scale operations at death's door to create a viable single entity can save struggling companies. Reducing overlapping responsibilities reduces costs, and expanding scale opens the possibility of satisfying larger customers. Interestingly, mergers among healthy enterprises are often more rancorous than those among weak companies because the latter know that their survival depends on collaboration.

The alternative to acquiring scale through a merger or a purchase is to build it within the company. Amazon.com, Inc., McDonald's Corporation, and Dell Computer Corporation have all chosen to enlarge their organizations themselves. Although mergers achieve scale more quickly, there are powerful reasons to prefer a growth strategy. After a merger, it is often difficult to combine distinct corporate cultures, operating procedures, and processes. Moreover, petty grievances, jealousies, and rivalries between the acquired and acquiring companies create frictions that can injure the combined organizations. Also, merger candidates have skeletons in their closets. Due diligence pares down, but doesn't eliminate, the number of unexpected surprises. Finally, acquisitions may be more expensive than internal growth.

If your company's annual sales are growing at the rate of 10 to 15 percent, our view is that you have no need to consider mergers or acquisitions to attain economies of scale. Your rate of ascent affords you the time to think about problems as they occur and make timely decisions on infrastructure-related issues. You aren't on the verge of outgrowing your facilities or your information technology.

However, when your growth exceeds 15 percent, problems begin. Your space becomes cramped, and some people have nowhere to work; you have hired new people, but your human resources department can't process them quickly enough; people make mistakes, such as keeping departed employees on the payroll. We have been asked to consult to companies with myriad, serious technology and processing issues. Some have not billed customers months after delivering their orders; others are incapable of turning out financial statements when suddenly creditors become aware and very anxious about a business's inability to manage explosive growth. If a company asks for an additional expansion of the working capital line less than 30 to 90 days after receiving the last amendment, a lending group may jump to the conclusion that management has bungled its way into a cash flow crisis.

Of course, the notion of enlarging a company to achieve economies of scale is hardly new. Henry Ford, John D. Rockefeller, and Adolphus Busch exploited their benefits of scale to build their businesses, both through internal growth and acquisition and merger. In the first decades of the twentieth century, in order to foster a free market and prevent monopolies, the U.S. government limited corporations' abilities to acquire competitors. But the globalization of commerce and the advent of the Internet have brought a modest relaxation of federal antitrust actions. Previously, prices tended to go up and quality and selection down after a merger, but more recently, competitiveness is tending to remain spirited even after giant mergers, because the resulting economies of scale allow consumer prices to be lowered.

The decision of whether to buy or build your way to larger scale depends on the availability and asking price of potential merger partners, as well as your organization's potential to develop internal opportunities for growth. How to use a cost advantage—whether to be a predator and seize market share or a profit maker and escalate earnings—depends on your organization's current strategy and the prevailing industry dynamics.

Still, the best-laid plans can go very wrong. For example, the merger of CDnow, Inc., and N2K, Inc., combined the two largest Internet music retailers. Together, they accounted for nearly 50 percent of online music sales (each had about 25 percent on its own). Independently, both experienced rapidly growing sales: N2K's sales jumped to $42 million in 1998 from $8 million in 1997, while CDnow's sales grew to $56 million from $17 million during the same period. But, together, they could not make any money: N2K lost $22 million, while CDnow lost $13 million. Their merger was designed for the sole purpose of gaining economies of scale. Inexplicably, management terminated one of the Web sites and absorbed all the business within CDnow. An alternative strategy would have been to maintain both sites in order to limit the entry of other merchants. That the venture had failed was obvious in the middle of 1999. CDnow is part of Bertelsmann eCommerce Group (BeCG), suggesting that the "merger" concept was a good one; it may have been the execution with N2K that was flawed. In fact, that was the Coca-Cola Company's view when it declared New Coke a success despite the fact that, in conventional terms, the product was a disappointment, but from Coke's viewpoint, it won more shelf space for the soft-drink giant.

As your company grows in size and reach, a constant danger is creating diseconomies of scale. They occur when communications become chaotic, decision making is deferred or transferred to dysfunctional departments, or leaders lose their vision and direction—any and all of which invite competitors to gain ground. These mistakes can cancel the advantages of size in no time and can actually drive the costs (both as a percentage of sales and per unit produced) of a large company above those of its smaller competitors.

Making wise decisions about scale and avoiding diseconomies depends to a great extent on how accurately the organization assesses its resources and the demand of its market. Sometimes, though, a company makes perfect assessments, and then, for no obvious reason, wanders off course.

Although, as a rule, you are more likely to maintain lower costs if you build a large facility, doing so may be a mistake if the predicted demand for the plant's output fails to materialize. Let's look at Toys "R" Us, Inc. (TRU). In a remarkable turnaround, the toy store chain, under the guidance of Charles Lazarus, moved out of bankruptcy in 1974 to become the world's number one toy seller, with more than 700 retail stores in the United States and 492 more internationally. But about five years ago, TRU's fortunes tumbled when nimble competitors, notably behemoth Wal-Mart Stores and Target Corporation, which has 975 outlets, may have outmaneuvered it. From 1998 to 2000, TRU embarked on a renewal effort that included closing unprofitable stores and unnecessary distribution centers and retrofitting the stores' interiors into a better-flowing design. This required a substantial write-off, which was accompanied by an additional write-off for excess inventories. The corporate focus changed dramatically. It was reestablished by February 2001, when the company said that it "had substantially completed its restructuring program." This may be true, but, unfortunately, income remains below the levels it achieved six years earlier.

Part of TRU's initial success can be attributed to a scale that allowed it to sell toys, diapers, and baby furniture at prices that few of its competitors could beat. With more than 1,500 stores, including its clothing and educational toy stores, worldwide TRU was positioned to dominate the entire children's retail business. But after overcoming its smaller adversaries, the press and financial analysts asserted that the company had focus and direction concerns. Its scope expansions sought to capitalize on its name, instead of on its reputation for low prices. Furthermore, it had operating difficulties that suggested diseconomies of scale. The problems were serious enough to begin to undermine its cost advantage.

In contrast with TRU, the Ford Motor Company offers an example of a successful expansion effort. In 1927, Ford built its mammoth River Rouge facility in Dearborn, Michigan, employing nearly 120,000 employees at that single site. Not only did River Rouge's output leave Ford's competitors in the dust, but the 2,000-acre plant was so efficient that the company's cost levels dropped well below those of other automakers, enabling Ford to slash its prices. As a result, consumer demand kept pace with the plant's increased output. River Rouge enabled a self-perpetuating cycle that was, simultaneously, profitable for Ford and beneficial for consumers: Ford increased its scale, in response to which its output grew, its costs declined , the savings were passed on to consumers in the form of lower prices, which made demand grow, increasing Ford's profit and stimulating larger economies of scale, and so on.

How Not to Lose the Scale Advantage

While few, if any, companies today can hope to replicate the River Rouge experience, they can nevertheless learn a valuable lesson from it. Growth will be achieved only if an eye is fixed on the most important metric of scale: cost as a percentage of gross revenue. This number is the basis of all other profit metrics, including the cost-per-unit reductions we discussed earlier in this chapter. Ignoring it explains why many companies get off track when they think about scale. Chief financial officers earn their keep by paying careful attention to this metric. We advise you to start financial quarterly reviews to make sure that as a company's top line grows, it is keeping a tight rein on costs. Otherwise, the benefits are lost, which may have happened at Boston Chicken, Inc., which later became Boston Market Corporation.

In the mid-1990s, Boston Market quickly established a reputation as a purveyor of good, fast, home-style food—an orientation with much appeal to a class of dual-income families who were always in a hurry. Small, productive, and efficient, the original 42 restaurants, which cost about $350,000 apiece, generated sales on average of $1.1 million. Following a public offering, another 1,100 restaurants opened, in the hope that expanding the chain would push costs down and economies of scale in purchasing, production, and management up. Space to sit down, which was a modification of the original concept, was added. When the company filed for bankruptcy, sales per unit were still $1.1 million, but the investment in each restaurant had grown reportedly to nearly $1.4 million.

Unproductive growth will not lead to scale. Out of 1,100 Boston Market restaurants, a large number were unprofitable. The ratio of sales to investment at the average restaurant reportedly declined from about 3.0 to only 0.8. Boston Market did not achieve scale; it merely spread itself too thin. In May 2000, McDonald's Corporation acquired 750 Boston Market restaurants out of bankruptcy with a plan to convert the locations into Golden Arches. But when it recognized the loyalty of Boston Market's customers, McDonald's, reportedly instead, spent time improving the stores' operations and kept its new acquisition in the chicken business.

Achieving the right scale is always a balancing act between sales, costs, and profits. During a vigorous expansion, the pressure from employees to increase costs are unrelenting. Your managers tell you that their sales are up 50 percent, but their budgets are up by only 10 percent, and they can't keep up. Can't they please add just a few more people? The problem is that the next quarter it is a few more people, and before you know it, your infrastructure is so swollen that reducing it requires outside help. The law of restructuring is that no one is going to relinquish any of his or her people voluntarily.

That sort of bloat can quickly cancel out any advantage won from economies of scale. It bears repeating that the best preventative measure is for the chief financial officer or chief executive officer to review costs every quarter. Then he or she can act immediately to keep costs at the desired percentage of gross profit or revenue.

In the service business, we monitor the client–service staff ratio closely to make sure that it stays within a certain percent of sales. Alarm bells ring when the numbers show that it has grown, say, 20 percent, but sales have increased just 10 percent. You see quickly that a reduction in force or a hiring freeze is in order.

Two of the cruelest truths in business are that large scale is no guarantee against failure, and a scale advantage doesn't last forever. Woolworth Corporation, for example, had an enormous scale advantage on its brand. In our personal view, the company missed some fundamental changes that were occurring in its business. Retailing has operated in cycles. First, there were mom-and-pop stores, followed by big urban department stores, after which catalogs appeared, then malls, which eventually became too much trouble to get to, hence the return of neighborhood shopping centers, and so on. At one time, the cycles were much longer than they are now, with customers' shopping preferences changing about every 50 years. Those periods shortened to 30, 20, 15 years. Now we have cycles of only 5 and 10 years in which one merchandising concept is favored over others. Woolworth may have missed the cyclical progression.

To some extent, Woolworth's scale insulated it from the need to keep pace with every shift in consumers' tastes, though some equally big organizations profited from staying abreast of transitions. That Woolworth had operated the same way for many successful years prevented it from acknowledging that its orientation was no longer working.

Woolworth's fate is what makes a board of directors decide to remove the chief executive and force a corporation to change. Some companies feel that changing top management will bring in fresh ideas. Large enterprises can lose their way by slowly developing into bureaucracies. As your company expands, you are expected, perhaps required, to have employment, environmental, and other policies in place. With scale comes the responsibility of guaranteeing that your foreign businesses are in compliance with U.S. laws. You need to create manuals that explain your standard operating procedures and clearly describe violations of organization policy. Lacking these rules and guidelines issues an open invitation to lawyers and other groups who are looking for an example of a business with uncaring attitudes and practices. Under such pressures, it is easy for companies to go too far to protect themselves from lawsuits or other attacks. Losing the quick and nimble feeling they had as smaller competitors, they begin to centralize decision making, which kills what is left of the entrepreneurial spirit.

One antidote is to keep the system decentralized. Many businesses are exploring the idea of giving vice-presidents the authority to make important decisions, rather than organizing that process within a corporate hierarchy. We think that can be beneficial even if some decisions override company policies that have been set in stone for years. It is one way of preventing a paper-choked bureaucracy, which often evolves once a corporation requires official manuals and policies to protect it.

In the end, your strategy for achieving scale and avoiding diseconomies, whether it is through mergers or internal growth, should be determined by your specific situation. So, we end this chapter with a relevant adaptation from the Oracle at Delphi: "Businessperson, know thyself—and your company."

CHAPTER 5

Handle Debt

Mark Twain was traveling in Europe when he opened a local paper and discovered his own obituary. He quickly took his pulse, then dispatched his famous response to the Associated Press: "The reports of my death are greatly exaggerated." This is exactly the right attitude for leaders of underperforming companies. Whatever doomsayers may say, nearly every sagging business has some kind of buried treasure waiting to be discovered by a creative, steadfast salvager. Indeed, this chapter is about the art of resuscitating struggling organizations by revealing the treasures they never knew they had.

Our tools for these Lazarus-like recoveries are restructuring, renegotiation, and merging—three words that we examine more carefully in the next section. (By no coincidence, they remind us of Mark Twain again. "A cauliflower," he said, "is a cabbage with a college education.") But first let's discuss the necessity of approaching a business crisis in the right spirit. Defeated managers can feel so hopeless that even if fresh opportunities shimmered in front of them, they would not see them. Accordingly, if their aspiring rescuers are to succeed, they should arrive free of doubt, confident the glass is half-full, and quite sure that usable riches lurk unnoticed in a dozen dark corners.

An almost infinite number of creative efforts have been aimed at finding previously unrecognized sources of wealth. Some years ago, we took on a client who was desperate for cash and appeared to have few, if any, assets. But, as a high-end publisher with wealthy subscribers, he was sitting on a plush asset—the names of those readers. Though he had considered selling his subscription list, we convinced him to keep it as a renewable resource. That some of the biggest names in luxury goods that coveted our client's affluent audience was proven when he raised almost half a million dollars by renting the list. Though, in time, the list grew stale, the rental income was a windfall that solved many of his short-term problems.

Remember Sasson designer jeans, now made by Azteca Production International, Inc.? When the company had very few assets and was in dire need of restructuring, its managers believed the name was a potent brand that should not be wasted on just one product line. They consulted a licensing agent, and within six months, they had more than 12 different licensing agreements for belts, shoes, perfume, hair products, jeans, T-shirts, handbags, and many other lines.

Another example is Fossil, Inc.'s Fossil watches, which considered its intangible assets as soon as the watch market started to turn down a couple of years ago. Unlike its many competitors, Fossil discovered that the "Fossil" brand was a valuable licensing commodity. Before long, it had significantly expanded its business by establishing other lines, including Fossil belts, wallets, and other leather goods.

You get the idea. And we have scores of other stories about intangible assets that turned out to be sources of very tangible new wealth. Those stories and others are just ahead.

Now let's clarify a few important terms, then use case studies from our experience to explain our general principles and guidelines for rethinking and remaking the business of any company at a crossroads.

Some Basic Definitions

Restructuring, renegotiation, and merging with other companies can benefit all organizations, but may be vital for those on the edge of failure.

- *Restructuring* transforms a company's balance sheet (assets and liabilities) or its ownership (equity). Financial restructurings extend debt repayments or change the debt's composition by converting one type of liability into another.

- *Renegotiation* means recontracting after the consummation of a deal. It takes place when a company is either, at its best, having surpassed all expectations, or, at its worst and facing life-threatening issues.

- *Mergers* combine two enterprises so they can benefit from synergies, larger scale, or the consolidation of an industry.

Restructuring includes countless financial practices, such as swapping equity shares for debt, issuing new shares with special privileges or a special price, and linking debt repayment to specific events. Its main objectives are to lower interest payments, reduce indebtedness, or postpone interest or principal repayment.

In contrast, renegotiation, which is more straightforward, seeks to amend a previous agreement so that it reflects altered circumstances. The existing pact may require a reduction in size, a delay, or a revision of price.

The nature of a merger varies widely depending on the relative strengths of the combining entities. An affiliation between a strong and a weak company is often, in fact, an acquisition, while one between two strong companies combines equals.

Restructuring

At first glance, there seem to be two distinct forms of restructuring: One is ongoing, retains stability, and prevents crises; the other is a crisis intervention intended to save a failing company. But closer inspection reveals that the difference is more in intensity and degree than in content or procedure.

Many of the best-run corporations are perpetually restructuring. Savvy chief executives know that stable periods are short, and change is measured in months or weeks, not years. In response to rapid shifts, they constantly adjust the numbers on their balance sheets, and reconsider their priorities, allocations, and percentages. The balance sheet and how cash is used invariably receive the most attention.

Those two priorities, debt and cash, are also the top priorities in troubled organizations, those that have no choice but to restructure. Though the crisis may have been in the making for a long time, it more likely was precipitated by a specific event, such as a significant drop in earnings or sales, at which point everyone—the company's officers, managers, board of directors, major creditors, and other stakeholders—starts closely examining the balance sheet and the company's cash flow.

In this barely controlled chaos, the people in its midst wonder if the situation can ever be resolved. The answer is yes, things can work out. Consider what happened at Philip Services Corporation a few years ago.

Based in Rosemont, Illinois, Philip Services had achieved revenues of $1.8 billion as a metal recycling and industrial service company. Its cash flow adequately covered its $1.1 billion debt until it discovered large unreported losses from unauthorized copper trades. Writing those losses off in mid-1998 made the company noncompliant with its bank loan covenants, the terms of which stipulated that Philip's interest payments could not exceed a certain percentage of its cash flow. A restriction of bank credit followed, as did a class action shareholder lawsuit and a management overhaul, together pushing Philip Services to a financial precipice.

Working with a steering committee of lenders, the company proposed a restructuring that incorporated aspects of a debt-for-equity exchange and also linked repayments to specific events. Exchanging $550 million of debt for 90 percent of the company's equity, the plan left existing shareholders with 10 percent ownership. The remaining debt would be repaid according to a formula based on excess cash flows and proceeds from asset sales.

That plan worked well for Philip Services, but it is important to remember that there are many philosophies on debt restructuring and the best use of cash that may have addressed Philip's situation differently, but just as appropriately. Some companies restructure debt long term, because they think that current interest rates will be hard to beat in the future. Others choose short-term debt in order to delay commitments, in the hope that the economy is going to change and financing will be less expensive, say, three years from now.

How to use cash is the biggest issue in an ongoing restructuring. Some corporations use it to buy back their own stock—you can't find a better investment than in your own company. Others pay dividends, which gives cash back to shareholders at a set return and declares that you can think of no better investment for their money.

Another school of thought maintains that if you restructure your balance sheet to reduce your debt in profitable times, you are prepared for tighter times when you might have to add it.

Amid all these various choices and perspectives, one ugly fact sits in your path like a junkyard dog: Excessive debt creates unremitting pressure from financial and trade creditors. Financial creditors harass management about delayed interest payments, violated debt covenants, sinking fund obligations, and early repayment obligations. They threaten to deny the company further credit, severing it from its bank, or to accelerate current obligations, making the organization repay its outstanding debt early. Trade creditors warn the struggling company about overdue balances and threaten to withhold further shipments. Losing the support of either your financial backers or your trade partners is devastating and is likely to destroy your entire enterprise.

Healthy corporations with excessive debt have to endure fewer assaults from creditors, but they lose some flexibility because of the relative shortage of equity on their balance sheets. Their inadequate equity may indicate that the capital-structure decisions—the relationship between debt and equity—that were appropriate at an earlier time are now outdated and need to be reconsidered because many things have changed. Or the company may have won market share but suffered severe financial strains in doing so, and now it needs to be recharged. A financial restructuring can neutralize previous errors and update the capital structure.

An example of a company that restructured creatively is EEX Corporation. Having discovered a significant oil field in the Garden Banks Block in the late 1990s, EEX needed cash to develop it, which proved difficult in the depressed oil industry of those years. Working to the company's disadvantage was its already high debt load and a nearly nonexistent equity market for oil stocks. To raise money, the company issued new stock at below-market price in a deal that called for Warburg, Pincus Equity Partners LP to buy $150 million of newly issued preferred shares and, in addition, to receive 21 million stock warrants (long-term options to buy common stock). The preferred stock would pay dividends in cash or shares at the discretion of the company. The warrants, exercisable at $12 per share, allowed Warburg, Pincus to acquire a significant ownership in the company at a low price, assuming the field developed as promised.

As in EEX's case, management usually—and preferably—initiates a restructuring. But sometimes the impetus comes from opportunists called vulture investors who purchase original positions at a steep discount. Commonly, such investors earn their name by their ruthless approach that can include dismissing management, merging with another company, or liquidating the enterprise. They want to realize a quick profit, then capture their next prey. To forestall settling with vultures, a company must hammer out a restructuring plan that benefits all stakeholders, construct a realistic scenario for its future performance, and put a talented management team in place. Performing these steps will encourage less rapacious creditors to become long-term stakeholders who are willing to wait for a fair return on their original investment. Alternatively, such creditors may wish to change their role and become owners.

Because in a restructuring crisis the company's goal is to convince creditors that forbearance and cooperation will maximize their investment return, establishing credibility is essential. Hence, companies are ill-advised to disguise their current condition and future potential.

A previous management team's less than honest approach will complicate the restructuring. An outside consultant may be better positioned to persuade creditors that they are more likely to receive their money if they allow a restructuring effort to succeed than if they force bankruptcy or liquidation. Furthermore, their chances dramatically improve if all involved parties understand the benefits of cooperation. Warnings or rumors of any drastic measure worsen matters by awakening passive creditors.

In the most prevalent type of restructuring, existing debt is sometimes exchanged for new equity shares, which transforms creditors into equity holders (or joint equity and debt holders if the exchange leaves some debt outstanding). From the cooperating creditor's point of view, equity has upside potential but is less secure than debt. From the company's perspective, less debt reduces interest and principal payments, but adding new equity holders may also reduce management's control over the corporation.

Of course, management wants to diminish its debt, but, in doing so, wants to relinquish as little financial stake and operational control as possible; that is, it wants to give up the fewest possible number of shares. Creditors, on the other hand, demand the authority to influence corporate policy as well as receive stock for their debts. It is critical that management maintain control, because creditors will be more willing to sell assets or to engage in a corporate combination (a merger or joint venture).

As we have discussed, restructuring efforts range from crisis management at one extreme to corporate transformation at the other. During a crisis-stage restructuring, the power resides disproportionately with the creditors. In a transformational restructuring, power is shared by creditors and management. If one party tries to bully the other, chances diminish for a productive working relationship. Regardless of who is perceived to have the upper hand, the adage "the sun can get a man to remove his jacket quicker than the wind" applies.

In a second frequently employed restructuring plan, new investors can be enticed with special preference equity shares—and there are many varieties. One sort of preference allows the holder to buy shares at a below-market price; another may give holders the option to buy more stock at a later date at a fixed price; still another offers preferred shares that pay cash interest now and can later be converted into regular stock. There are also preference shares that are, in fact, a second class of equity in which the number of votes per share exceeds that of the regular stock. The multiple-vote feature enables debt holders to take control of a company by converting a relatively small dollar amount of debt.

A third type of restructuring links debt repayment or interest payments to specific financial events, such as the sale of an asset or a positive cash flow quarter. Called contingent restructuring, such pay-as-you-can agreements alleviate, to some extent, the fierce day-to-day pressures for repayment or improved performance. For the creditor, contingent restructuring represents a promise that it will benefit as the company's balance sheet improves. Negotiations among all parties establish the "events" that will trigger repayments. Such an arrangement will work best if all involved realize that they can't squeeze water from a rock: If creditors must give the company enough time to replenish its resources before draining them again to service debt, the corporation must realize that creditors aren't charitable organizations.

Renegotiation

Few terms in the business lexicon are as stigmatized as *renegotiation*. When they hear a request to renegotiate, some people dig in their heels and refuse to participate; others cooperate, but only reluctantly.

Resisting a renegotiation is understandable in ordinary times, but it can be self-defeating during a crisis. When the Phoenix Effect is absolutely essential, the company's only alternatives are bankruptcy or liquidation, both of which are extremely costly. Expenses include legal fees, lost goodwill, and disruptions of strategic and technical planning and development. Often, a better deal can be arranged through a renegotiation that minimizes legal fees and disruption to the business.

Consider the case of Northeast Utilities Services Company, which is based in West Springfield, Massachusetts. Like other large electricity providers, Northeast relies heavily on borrowed funds to finance its extensive array of power plants. In 1998, $313 million of its debt was a borrowing package funded by an 11-bank consortium headed by Citibank N.A. These bank lines of credit usually aren't protected against default with assets pledged as security; instead, they link strict lending covenants to the borrower's operations, the purpose of which is to prevent the borrower from taking on more risk than the lender feels comfortable with.

Having accepted the lending syndicate's terms, Northeast found itself operating on the edge of violating several loan covenants as a consequence of unanticipated financial exigencies. In particular, it was close to violating an interest coverage requirement (the comparison of its income to its interest obligations) and its equity level obligation. Penalties for these transgressions range from minor to severe. In the worst case, the financial institution accelerates the loan and demands immediate repayment.

Fortunately, the banks agreed to relax the lending covenants to ease Northeast Utilities' situation. The bankers in this case may have compromised to prevent the utility from changing banks or for many other good reasons. One is that the utility was requesting only minor adjustments: for the common equity level to shrink from a requirement of 32 percent to 31, and the expected long-run ratio of operating income to interest expense to narrow from 2.5:1 to 2.0:1. In addition, Northeast pointed to a recently reconditioned and reopened nuclear power plant that would, according to the utility, provide a significant new revenue stream without posing public safety risks.

It was a renegotiation that worked because it satisfied both parties' mutual needs. The company maintained its credit facility, while the lender not only retained a huge client but was reassured about that client's future health.

The relationship between Northeast Utilities and the banking syndicate represents one of many ways a renegotiation can be worked out. Sometimes, the process can be most useful if initiated during a profitable time when a company achieves unexpected success, as opposed to a troubled time when creditors are more concerned. As we will see, the former was the situation when Netscape Communications Corporation asked InfoSeek Corporation to renegotiate their arrangement.

Sitting down to change the terms of a deal makes even old corporate friends suspicious and wary, but overcoming this initial distrust transforms the process into an opportunity. Listening to your client's needs creates a chance to enhance a profitable relationship. Good, ongoing communication can unsnarl most problems, unless the renegotiation's aim is to terminate the relationship.

Perhaps the toughest aspect of a renegotiation is that, unlike a negotiation, the relationships are asymmetric. In the latter, both sides stand to gain, whereas in the former, one party will benefit at the expense of the other. An able negotiator helps the losing party perceive that, in fact, it does gain something: Perhaps it will retain a desirable portion of the original contract, or get a few sweetened terms incorporated into a new one.

An example of how this works occurred in the late 1990s when Netscape renegotiated its deal with InfoSeek. The two companies had an agreement that called for InfoSeek, a search engine, to pay Netscape Netcenter a fixed fee for every search request that the latter forwarded to the former. By 1999, after a dramatic upswing in the popularity of the Internet and Netcenter, it became clear to Netscape that the rates it was charging InfoSeek were far below what the service was worth. So Netscape asked to renegotiate, and InfoSeek agreed.

From the start, the spirit of the renegotiations was positive. That a continued relationship would be beneficial to both parties was clear even though Netscape wanted to raise its rates. In the new agreement, Netscape would direct just 5 percent of its search requests (down from 15 percent) to InfoSeek (unless the user requested a particular search engine). Moreover, InfoSeek agreed to pay Netscape 20 percent more per unit for this traffic.

Though these renegotiations reduced InfoSeek's accessibility to Netscape's clients, they allowed a mutually profitable partnership to continue. They also spurred Info-Seek to widen its business: During the course of the discussions, InfoSeek diversified its search request providers to include ABCNEWS.com, ESPN.com, and the Microsoft Network.

We can break down the stages of a renegotiation, like the one between Netscape and InfoSeek, into three steps. First, the contractor (the party initiating the discussion—Netscape, in our example) discusses candidly with the negotiator why the existing contract is problematic. This step focuses on coaxing the contract holder to the table and defining the agenda of that first meeting. Second, the negotiator explains to the contract holder precisely what the contractor needs and outlines various ways for attaining it. Finally, a new contract that shrinks, delays, or reprices the original one is agreed upon. Following these steps can promote mutual interests in both companies' future opportunities, which will certainly boost the renegotiation's probability of success.

No matter how dark things look as you work your way through this process, remember that renegotiation will succeed if each side perceives an opportunity to cut its losses, either actual or projected. In the immortal words of Sonny Corleone in the first *Godfather* film: "Offer them a deal they cannot refuse." For our purposes, offering "a deal they cannot refuse" means offering a deal that is better than no deal at all.

Getting the Best Deal

All parties involved in a renegotiation work hard to achieve a positive outcome; results like Netscape's and Northeast Utilities' don't just happen. Behind all such agreements, including restructures and mergers, are endless days of bargaining and negotiating. Remember, the stakes are very high. We are challenging ideas people have held and assumed to be true for a long time, and we are doing so in a context that involves huge sums of money.

Given the effort you expend, nothing is worse than ending this process with the feeling that you could have gotten more. In these negotiations, it is critical that you gain and retain the upper hand; nearly everyone's assumption is that you are dealing from a position of weakness. Therefore, in the next several pages, we will walk through a restructuring step-by-step, covering many of the practical details.

From the day it becomes clear that your business has a problem, you need to stop the creditors from hounding you. In a renegotiation, things are seldom what they seem, and never less so than in financial negotiations. The balance of power shifts without warning and will be more unsteady if you are dealing with an experienced creditor, such as a bank or your bondholders. Just when you think you are solidly in control, you find yourself helplessly suspended in midair.

This is true, too, for the creditors.

When we represent a company in these negotiations, we assume the initiative in our first meeting with the lenders. Perhaps we open by thanking everyone for coming, emphasizing how much we want to work together; we will refer to the "interesting few weeks since we released the earnings" and express the corporation's concern. The idea is to persuade everyone that we are on top of the situation and have taken all the obvious first steps: that is, "We've sold the company airplane; grounded the cars; aggressively cut marketing and advertising costs; and we are in the process of cutting all controllable expenses." The rule here is to beat creditors to the basics.

At this stage, we signal the creditors that if we aren't careful, the situation could be more chaotic and complicated; we subtly point out that we need each other and, then, give the counterpunch. You might consider saying something along the lines of this: "As you can imagine, we very much want to keep the sales force in place as well as those whose responsibility it is to protect the assets." That is the counterpunch. So quickly go on to say, "Of course, the people in the accounting department who collect the receivables and know what's good and what's going to be tough are being wooed by the headhunters; we are trying to figure out how we can prevent our staff from leaving during this restructuring." We sometimes add that "we're reexamining the inventory to decide what course of action is needed, if anything."

Never move beyond hinting at this stage. That the bank needs the existing management team to guide this process is the point we are trying to make. If you overdo it, the creditors may feel misled. They may feel that you are too aggressive and distrustful and that you think their collateral is suspect—they may feel you are threatening their control. But if you strike the right balance, they think that your team is dealing with the issues and knows something they haven't thought about.

Most of the lenders want quick settlements. Though they talk tough about liquidation, it is rarely their goal. However, that fact isn't always obvious to the officers of a troubled company, who are vulnerable to being intimidated and should never enter negotiations without expert counsel.

One ploy the banks use, which most likely the company's executives won't spot as a decoy, is intended to throw a chief executive off balance by switching the tempo. The chief executive thinks she is there to discuss restructuring the debt, until a bank negotiator interrupts a line of thought to ask her, "Is it possible we could get a copy of your liquidation analysis to compare with our own?" Quietly, the chief executive panics. It is an old trick to remind her who is holding the gold. The bank, which has probably already decided that a new loan would be the best course, employs this scare tactic, hoping it will stop the chief executive from pounding the table when she hears the new loan's terms or interest points. The creditors want her to feel grateful to get out of there alive and with the loan.

Sometimes a bank demands collateral for a loan, and a chief executive quickly agrees just to end the crisis. But this tips the seesaw back in the bank's favor. The chief executive had not realized that she held some gold as long as the collateral wasn't pledged to the bank. Now she has lost that leverage.

That a chief executive has a professional negotiator whom he trusts and whom he lets do the talking is absolutely vital. One advantage is that the professional knows the opposition. If you are in the business long enough, you learn who are the real cutthroats, who are the bluffers, and who have seriously bad attitudes. With a seasoned professional with whom you face real mental combat, remind the chief executive not to be goaded into giving away information that you want to use to your advantage later. You don't want to spend all your bullets while the other guy is wearing an armored vest.

We advise our clients never to put all their cards on the table in a negotiation. Keep the other side guessing.

Never test the water with both feet at once: It may be over your head. And never, we urge them, miss an opportunity to shut up. Despite their certainty that the loss of one of their biggest accounts is common knowledge, they would be foolish to volunteer that information without a solution. If they do, word will spread, which could affect the cash flow projections disastrously. While it is always possible to release information, it is impossible to call it back.

The following example of a negotiation involved a business that produced home decorations and other bric-a-brac. It was a household name among upper-middle-class women, and it was having horrendous cash flow problems. We will let Carter tell his team's story.

The directors were worried about the CEO's capacity to represent the company at the negotiations; their anxieties were justified, and he was replaced.

The new CEO wasn't up-to-date on the events, so we made sure that he was never available for crucial meetings. We let the bankers know that he couldn't be there, but I was authorized to represent him.

After the preliminaries, the bank opened the negotiations with a standard decoy of asking how quickly the company could be liquidated. We thought "guys, don't snow the snowman." We said, "If enough trucks were available, we could probably liquidate in a day; we'll back the loaded trucks up to your branches and park them on your front lawn." Beyond a doubt, that tipped the seesaw, because management knew how to move these products; the bank did not. If the company didn't cooperate, the bank would get only 10 cents on the dollar, but it could see five times that amount if it bought management's goodwill.

We informed the bank that unless we got immediate relief, the company would have to file for bankruptcy, and then, it is a "jump ball." The bank called our bluff, and we filed. But, just as in jujitsu, we gained the advantage by falling back. What were the assets worth in liquidation? If the company were to reorganize, who would run it? Again, in that situation, the bank needed the management team more than it needed the bank. The negotiations became very tense.

Nearly every approach we know was brought to bear in those meetings. We told them that we were also looking at our various options. When asked what those were, my answer was: "Well, of course, as you know, a company in our position has a number of options and, at this point, we haven't yet completely decided. We're waiting for a signal from you as to whether or not you are willing to work with us." As we said earlier, never reveal exactly what you're thinking. Let them guess about what those options might be.

We have also used "the walkout," which is useful if you aren't making any progress, or if you want the other party to consider what could happen if you didn't return. Walking out is most effective if you can leave with an abrupt comment that throws the other side off balance. In these negotiations, when someone from the bank said, "We're going to need the collateral before we go forward," I said, "Gentlemen, with that, this meeting is over. We'll get back to you," leaving the bank people defensively squabbling. From my experience on the other side, I guessed their conversation went something like this: "Jeez, Jim, I thought we were going to ease the company into that topic. You got that guy excited." "He wasn't angry," his associate may have shot back. "He just said the meeting was over."

If we either needed a time-out or thought we had progressed as far as we could for that day, I would say, "We're going to stop, reflect on today's discussion, review our options, and get back to you," leaving matters ambiguous.

The outcome was that the bank gave up the idea of liquidation; we undertook a massive renegotiation of the entire loan agreement, and the company was successfully reorganized and back in business.

Still, that wasn't quite the end of it. You might think there are only four aces in a deck of cards, but there's always one somebody hasn't yet played. When the bank thought it was all over, I said, "Okay, we've negotiated the debt. Now, my management team and I will agree to stay if the bank will underwrite us a year's severance pay if this turnaround doesn't work out." And it did.

As we said, negotiations are never what they seem.

Mergers

In the previous chapter, we examined mergers as opportunities to reduce costs. Here we want to focus briefly on the strategic options associated with mergers, which to a large extent depend on whether the merger candidates are strong or weak.

When a weak company merges with a stronger one, the company needing help can, at a stroke, pick up sharper management, improved performance, access to financing, and entrée to a larger customer base. The merger of two weak companies can also work, provided that the combined enterprise has a positive profit margin and looks to be an acceptable risk to lenders. A merger can only benefit a weak business if operating efficiencies, product synergies, or other marketing, financial, or managerial advantages are achieved.

If healthier companies that are engaged in a Phoenix Effect exercise merge, they do so to penetrate new markets, avoid obsolescence, create a bigger enterprise through synergies, and perhaps solve management succession concerns, as well as to combine technologies, resources, and workforces.

Strong companies, in our experience, are often overly optimistic about the advantages of merging with weaker ones, and their high hopes are dashed. One reason is that the latter aren't always entirely forthcoming about their flaws. This is not to say that all weak companies should be avoided, but strong companies should move cautiously in such mergers, conduct thorough due diligence investigations, and formulate realistic business plans for the combined organization.

Of course, *strong* and *weak* are imprecise and relative terms, as the following three examples of recent mergers illustrate. Arguably each of the three involves a strong partner and a weak partner; but it could also be argued that Kia Motors Co., Ltd. and Hyundai Corporation are two weak companies, while BankBoston Corporation and BayBanks, Inc. are two strong ones. In any event, all three examples put flesh on the merger principles we've just discussed.

■ Kia Motors, one of South Korea's big three automakers, failed in 1997 following a rapid slowdown in the Korean economy. Hastening its demise was economic weakness in Indonesia, where Kia was planning a $1 billion joint venture with the son of former Indonesian President Suharto. With debts totaling $6.7 billion, Kia sought to restructure its loans or get new financing, but these efforts were unsuccessful, and the government eventually nationalized Kia Motors.

Kia's niche—small inexpensive sport-utility vehicles (SUVs)—had considerable potential and the company attracted four bidders: Ford Motor Company, plus three Korean automakers—Hyundai Motor, Daewoo Motor Co., Ltd., and Renault Samsung Motors Co. Ford, which already owned 16.9 percent of Kia, won the bid, but the South Korean government's reluctance to let foreign interests control one of its key companies yoked Kia with Hyundai. This merger ensured the continued production and sale of Kia's products, at least for the immediate future.

■ In 1997, when an investor group paid about $18 million to save Business Express Airlines (BEA) from bankruptcy, it didn't look as though the group was making a particularly promising deal. Keeping a small airline solvent is difficult under the best of circumstances, considering the competition from major airlines.

Under the new plan, BEA, operating as BEX, a Delta Air Lines Connection commuter airline, signed a code-share agreement with AMR Corporation's American Airlines and began selling its flights as both Delta Air Lines, Inc. and American. To almost everyone's surprise, American found that it was gaining more passengers from BEA than it had expected.

American now had something else to worry about. It feared that Delta might try to buy BEA. In December 1998, American bought BEA for $55 million. In addition to eliminating a competitive threat, American hoped to achieve major efficiency gains by fully integrating the two lines.

■ Before the two got together, BankBoston and Bay-Banks were two very strong but very different institutions, each with its own distinct personality. BankBoston Corporation was a super-regional bank with assets of $73.5 billion employing 25,000 people. Founded in 1784, it was the nation's oldest commercial bank. In contrast, BayBanks, with $12 billion of assets and 5,800 employees, was a 70-year-old institution that had become the dominant consumer bank in Massachusetts.

Though each bank was strong in different market segments, a Phoenix Effect analysis suggested that both institutions needed to round out their scope and market strengths by finding a partner with complementary strengths. BankBoston, a business and government bank that was dominant throughout New England, specialized in high technology, energy, and media and communications. BayBanks, the major bank in Massachusetts for small businesses and consumers, had a wide network of ATMs.

The marriage was made. BankBoston acquired BayBanks, rounded out its product offerings, and became the dominant consumer bank in the commonwealth. Motivating the merger, too, was the boost it gave to BankBoston's effort to remain independent. At the time, the super-national banks were on the prowl for their own merger candidates. The BayBanks's affiliation, though small of its own accord, made BankBoston much more expensive, hence more difficult to purchase. However, a year later the combined bank was itself acquired by Fleet Financial Group, Inc., to create a financial-services colossus, FleetBoston Financial Corporation.

Merger strategy must always acknowledge U.S. antitrust laws as wild cards. While the Clayton Antitrust Act restricts mergers among major players in the same market, its limits are blurry, and the courts have shown latitude if the merger is an enterprise's last hope. The tactic of legally exploiting this flexibility has become known as the "failing-firm defense." During the Great Depression, the U.S. Supreme Court ruled in the case of *International Shoe v. FTC* (Federal Trade Commission) that acquiring a financially troubled competitor didn't violate the Clayton Antitrust Act. While later legislation has restricted this decision, regulators are still willing to permit desperation or failing-firm defense mergers. Their rationale is that if the failing organization will otherwise vanish, a merger will at least preserve some jobs.

The right merger partner should be obvious; if it isn't, the negotiations may prove lengthy and difficult. Sometimes a strong company waits until a weaker one fails so that it can buy its assets out of bankruptcy court. Although that ploy may make sense when hard assets, such as oil wells or aircraft, are involved, it is extremely risky, especially if customer goodwill is a major asset.

Remember, price is always negotiable in a merger. Obviously, when a weak organization combines with a strong one, the weaker company's shareholders receive less than they wish. In fact, it isn't uncommon for these transactions to occur without the acquirer paying a premium over the market price; the merger may even occur below the market price level. If the merger was well conceived, the shareholders' initial disappointment should gradually be replaced with gratification as profits of the merged company rise.

Mergers invariably evoke the image of the big greedy enterprise gobbling up the brave little company, a view that dovetails with the inaccurate myth that business is a jungle. That enterprises are born, live for a while, and die; that management comes and goes; that business plans fall apart; that stock prices deflate like old balloons; that entropy rules—these things make the business world look cold and cruel. But the energy that drives it is never lost, it is always there waiting to be tapped. In good times there is so much energy in the air, you can't fail to catch some of it. When the economy falters, you have to work harder to channel the energy your organization needs to prosper.

The strategies we have examined in this chapter— restructuring, renegotiation, and merger—are often thought of as defensive maneuvers, stratagems to avert failure. In fact, they are three Phoenix Effect methods for rejuvenating your enterprise. They are the business world's forces of renewal and should be used as such.

CHAPTER 6

Get the Most from Assets

Most failing companies are about to run out of the indispensable fuel of a going business—working capital. But such a crisis is nearly always a result, not a cause, of a long series of previous follies, typically stemming from a faulty business model.

Even a good business model isn't insulated from unexpected changes: A competitor suddenly emerges with a better, cheaper, faster solution; new laws or regulations shrink the market for your product; consumer tastes swerve in another direction; or the economy plunges. As a result, huge amounts of inventory back up in the warehouse, tying up equally large amounts of working capital. But this didn't originate as a working-capital problem. The real issue is that customers aren't buying the product in the quantities or at a price that could make the company viable.

Most of the working-capital crises we see can be compared to the final stages of a fatal disease. While respiratory failure may be the technical cause of the patient's death, the cancer that caused it has been doing its lethal work for months or years.

One common manifestation of a working-capital crunch is when a company decides to buy rather than lease brick-and-mortar assets, then sinks considerable capital into a new state-of-the-art distribution center. With most of its money tied up in the new building and equipment, the enterprise is hard-pressed for cash to pay its current expenses and bills, let alone for funding ambitious programs to market its products. This organization has genuine cash flow problems. Fortunately, it can be salvaged. We discuss how in this chapter.

First, in this case, the business is sound and, except that it invested too much money in building and equipment, runs perfectly well. Hence, odds are it will emerge from its working-capital crisis as long as a suitable way for it to derive cash or liquid assets from the bricks and mortar is found.

The Wisdom of Regular Checkups

A basic rule for all businesses, whether they are booming, busting, or recovering from a financial stroke, is that if you carefully follow the ebb and flow of your working capital, you are very likely to spot problems in time to prevent serious damage, if not avert them entirely. Managing working capital astutely is far more than bean counting; it can work as an early warning system informing you that profit margins aren't what they should be and need immediate attention.

If your organization's key working-capital ratios, such as current assets to current liabilities, fall outside its industry's benchmark norms, then something may be wrong, and you need to examine the situation further to determine the cause.

In our experience, nothing is more effective for working-capital management than regular checkups.

Too often, by the time organizations call us for help, it is too late for a simple intervention, and major surgery, sometimes an amputation, is the only hope. That is why we urge quarterly working-capital reviews—if not monthly, or even weekly when the situation is critical.

Frequently, the first words we hear from the CEO are this classic line: "We've got inventory that no one wants, receivables that no one can collect, and cash that no one can find." We see disastrous situations, and we don't yet have the numbers that would lead us to suggest fixes—that is, if any can help.

We are the first to admit that keeping track of your receivables, inventory, and payables can be unglamorous work. But, like changing your car's oil or dusting your furniture, it must be done. In fact, if performing those tasks becomes exciting, you are in trouble.

Mismanagement can occur in the blink of an eye when business circumstances change. Consider what happens when signs point to an economic slowdown.

That it is hard to procure bank financing or float a bond issue in a slowing economy means that maintaining high liquidity is very important. When markets slow, you want your investment in inventory and receivables to be as low as possible, ready for a sharp retraction of customer buying. Fear certainly can perpetuate a slowdown. Faced with the possibility of declining sales, some retailers panic and, instead of ordering 50,000 units a month, they order 10,000. In an economic slowdown, when purchasing habits change so dramatically so quickly, a kind of mass hysteria ensues. The sudden halt on buying triggers a domino effect in the supply chain. Even if this is irrational, you don't want to get caught in the downdraft, so be as liquid as possible.

A company that doesn't monitor its working capital very closely during slowdowns tends to be unable to maintain a comfortable middle ground between a state of complacency and one of crisis. Typically, the situation becomes urgent when the financial officer wakes up (around the 10th of the month, when bills are due) and realizes that the company doesn't have the money to make the quarterly payment of bond interest, fund payroll by Friday, and satisfy the construction company in Florida that requests another large draw. She informs the president, who asks, "How can that be?" The financial officer explains that the money is trapped in inventory and receivables because of the slowdown. Next, creditors start to constrain credit limits, and that is how a working-capital crisis develops.

To be sure, the best organizations try to manage their working capital very carefully. One method many use to help avoid surprises is to compose a one-page summary of working-capital positions for the chief executive to study at scheduled intervals. If a number or ratio is approaching the danger zone, it will appear on the summary against the benchmark, enabling the chief executive to authorize remedial action. A small problem with working assets can quickly grow out of control and become a disaster.

Minding the Nuts and Bolts

Louis Pasteur told us that "chance favors the prepared mind." Conversely, misfortune strikes those who neglect their ordinary tasks. Companies need routinely to perform a range of daily chores—all tedious and essential. They include paying bills, ordering inventories, extending credit, and maintaining a sufficient level of short-term financing. Organizations that skimp on these responsibilities in favor of, say, high-tech glamour or elaborate marketing risk turning minor stumbles into major falls.

Businesses, like people, are usually in debt. Long-term debt need not be paid in full for years; other debt is a current liability that must be repaid faster, usually within a year. Long-term debt may be secured (protected by a pledged asset, such as securities or a building) or unsecured. Liabilities must be paid according to terms worked out between the parties.

The two most common current liabilities are accounts payable, which are owed to vendors, and notes payable, usually due to a bank. Typically, an organization owes money to many separate vendors (though in most cases, the largest five account for 50 percent or more of the total owed). In contrast, borrowed funds often come from a single bank.

Corporate assets, like liabilities, can be long term or short term. Long-term assets, such as plants or property, traditionally comprise the majority of total assets, with current assets constituting a smaller percentage.

Cash, accounts receivable, and inventories are the major current assets. Cash must be available to pay bills, so it is kept in a liquid, interest-bearing account. Accounts receivable is the name for the money your customers owe you; in fact, it is credit that you have extended to customers that has not yet been collected. Inventories include raw materials (yarn and integrated circuits are examples), works-in-progress (partially built products), and finished goods awaiting sale and shipment.

Net working capital, which means the liquid assets available to cover your short-term obligations, is determined by adding your current assets and subtracting your current liabilities. How do you know if yours is at a healthy level? Check your current ratio—meaning current assets divided by current liabilities. Depending on norms in your industry, the ideal ratio is roughly 1.5 to 2.5.

Some inventories and accounts receivable may not be converted into cash easily, so including them at full value may exaggerate the amount of net working capital that is actually available. Accordingly, cautious accountants discount inventories and receivables by a certain fraction before determining how fully liabilities are covered.

A situation in which your current ratio excludes illiquid items, such as inventory, is sometimes called an "acid test" ratio, since it focuses on truly liquid assets. In that case, the asset-liability ratio should be about 1:1.

The importance of managing working capital can't be overstated. You may have great products and terrific resources, but if you stop paying attention to current assets and current liabilities, your business is headed for the sick list.

Conversely, a recovering company has to concentrate more intensely than ever on managing its working capital. That was especially vital during the recent boom when labor was scarce and it was hard to find qualified chief financial officers and controllers. Now that the job market has loosened, strive to protect yourself against the disasters that can result from hiring people who don't appreciate the vital nature of managing a recovering enterprise's working assets.

Managers must take three actions so that a company can renew itself:

1. Uncover existing errors and omissions and get out of denial.

2. Implement accounting controls to avoid further damage.

3. Regain working-capital control.

Our survey of turnaround managers confirmed the obvious fact that nearly every company in crisis has a working-capital problem. What was startling was our discovery that virtually none of these businesses had developed a system of cash flow management or valuable accounting data. We are referring to accounting information that includes product-cost data (how much labor, material, and overhead are used in each product), break-even data (on fixed and variable cost), and a variance analysis that looks for efficiencies and inefficiencies by comparing actual costs against a standard.

Alert working-capital managers can provide a valuable predictive function by preparing cash budgets that warn of impending cash shortfalls. A cash budget describes the expected inflow and outflow of cash that is used for, but not limited to, wages, supplier outlays, receipts from customers, bond repayments, and dividends. Unsurprisingly, 90 percent of businesses in crisis have no cash flow management.

We believe that nothing substitutes for the crisp, unadorned financial reporting that a concise cash forecast—or the one-page working-capital summary that we suggested earlier—provide. If you use the summaries, ask your outside auditors to specify what such a report should include, but don't stop there. Ask them for industry guidelines so you can see if your working-capital ratios fall within a healthy range. If your turnover in inventory is outside your industry benchmark, something may be wrong. You may be missing customer orders. Your auditors (or accountants or other professional advisers) can help you get back to the right level for receivables, aging of receivables and payables, availability of cash, and the other working-capital items on your one-page report.

The working-capital report will be even clearer and more useful if problem areas are highlighted, say in bold red. At a glance, you can see where any current numbers are abnormal. For instance, if your receivables are outside the industry's standards—say, their aging is out over 90 days—then you need to talk with your salespeople and your receivable-collection clerk to understand these delays in getting paid.

The one-page working-capital report enables you to focus on problems very quickly. You don't need prolonged conversations with all your key people to find out what is going on in the business.

Now, let's look more closely at the components of working capital. Only by doing so can we fully understand the factors that make for its good (and bad) management. We will start with current assets and current liabilities, move on to three basic rules for effective working-capital management, and end with a few corporate examples.

Current Assets

Cash, by itself, has limited earning power (typically, the interest paid by a bank on checking accounts). Therefore, in most circumstances, your cash holdings should be minimal. On the other hand, bills usually can't be paid with any other assets, so it is advisable to maintain at least a modest cash account.

Organizations with weak financial-control systems often lose track of their cash. As a result, they either bounce checks or hold on to more cash than they need. The first mistake incurs bank fees, angers suppliers, and gives lending institutions the impression that the company's managers are inept. Equally damaging is the second mistake, which leaves too many asset dollars doing nothing. As good managers know, both mistakes are avoidable.

The best way to ensure that you have the right amount of cash on hand is to make a cash budget for the year ahead, by day, week, or month. On your budget calendar, anticipated expenditures (taxes, insurance, payroll, vendors, etc.) should be set against estimates of funds to be received. This juxtaposition will reveal when cash shortfalls or surpluses are likely to occur. With a budget calendar, an organization is prepared to obtain a bank credit line that covers the largest predictable shortfalls. The actual amount of the credit line will vary as the company collects receipts (reducing the line) and pays its bills (increasing the line).

Before the cash level gets too low or too high, a control mechanism should sound an alarm, warning managers to avoid both a cash crisis and a surplus. With a prearranged bank lending line, cash shortfalls are automatically covered.

When cash builds up, it is impractical to convert it into productive assets, such as inventories or machines, for just a short time. In such cases, a good use of surplus funds is to pay down the bank line of credit (thus reducing interest charges). Some financial institutions offer special corporate checking accounts that will automatically sweep your surplus funds out of deposit accounts and apply them to paying down your bank loans. Very small businesses rely on credit cards for short-term borrowing needs, repaying the loan when funds are available.

Short-term business loans are now available through corporate credit cards, such as the American Express Company's small business card program, which offers a free "Platinum Corporate Optima" card. Not to be outdone, Visa International, Inc. has introduced a small business line of credit that is attached to regular credit cards.

If you compare interest rates as well as administrative and application fees, credit cards are cheaper than some commercial loans. Certain vendors prefer them; they make it unnecessary to open credit accounts with multiple vendors; and credit card balances can be repaid in full at any time.

The stories you hear about independent movie producers funding projects with 5 or 10 credit cards are true. Other small businesses also use them for funding, as well. The downside is that too much easy debt carries the risk of bankruptcy. Moreover, the cards' interest rates exceed those of the banks. An additional issue is an ethical one. A business that opens new credit card accounts knowing they are being used to fund a project that is likely to fail is behaving unethically.

Accounts receivable are money your customers owe you for whatever they bought from you. If they pay by check or credit card, the purchase is entered as an "account receivable" on your balance sheet and remains there until you collect the money.

Although finance organizations prosper by providing loans to customers who want to buy high-ticket items, the producers and suppliers on the other side of the transaction prefer cash to a receivable. Cash is money in the bank, while receivables are monies that you may collect at some future date if the buyer doesn't default on the obligation. Cash can also be converted into other assets at any time, but receivables are tied up until they are actually collected. If an organization urgently needs cash, it can turn to "factors," or banks that buy receivables at a discount, perhaps at 94 or 95 percent of face value.

Business is full of cruel stories about companies caught in terrible cash binds and forced to unload their receivables at fire sale prices. Time isn't your friend when you need cash and you are trying to collect on receivables.

We have had desperate calls on a Wednesday from businesses that couldn't make payroll on Friday, and the bank group wasn't willing to meet with us until Monday. All we could do was take our client's top 10 receivable accounts and call the chief financial officers of each of those 10 companies. Once we reached these people, we would say, "You owe us X amount of money. We know it isn't due for another 15 days, but we will give you a discount if you pay right now."

Why the chief financial officer? Remember Willie Sutton, the famous 1930s bank robber? Asked why he robbed banks, Willie said, "Because that's where the money is."

If anyone knows where a company's money is, it is the chief financial officer. He or she is the decision maker and knows the value of time and money. We don't have to explain the concept of a discount to him or her. A good chief financial officer knows exactly where his or her company's cash stands. Why waste time talking to the president, who is probably more interested in the sales and customer side of the business?

A good chief financial officer will get right down to brass tacks and ask: "What kind of discount are you thinking about?" And so the negotiating begins. It is really an auction of the receivable, which ends when the chief financial officer hits a point where he or she feels it is foolish not to wire you the money. Often we have saved companies and bought a little bit of breathing room by giving as much as a 10 or 15 percent discount in return for immediate cash. Now, of course, this is a dangerous game because you have signaled to them that something is amiss in your organization. But in matters of survival, companies don't have the luxury of complaining about the bitterness of the medicine that saves their lives.

Although cash is king, a receivables collector sometimes has to accept whatever he can get. We once pursued a clothing manufacturer who couldn't pay our client because he had no cash. In desperation, he offered us 10,000 men's belts, and with the same feeling, we accepted. We contacted a major liquidator who immediately found a retailer who was about to order a large quantity of belts for his stores. We converted one person's inventory into someone else's cash.

But happy endings are rare in this game.

Given such customers, we sometimes wonder why companies extend credit at all. Of course, each decides if credit will be available to its customers and, if so, on what basis. Terms range from strict "cash only, no credit" to very liberal "as long as you need to pay" options. Credit is offered to match or outdo competitors, or because the customer is unable to afford a cash purchase. Large, well-capitalized companies have credit subsidiaries whose business is to profit from the extension of credit.

Usually, though, organizations are wise to remember that they aren't in the credit business and should use it only to stimulate sales or to remain competitive. In some cases, credit policy becomes an integral part of an organization's Phoenix Effect effort. While tightening credit may alleviate a cash flow problem, a more liberal credit policy can tip the scales and generate sales.

Credit terms define the contractual arrangement between the seller and buyer, including payment terms, interest rate policies, and cash-payment discounts. Payment schedules may be very tight, as short as one day; others may be extraordinarily generous, perhaps as long as a year. Interest rates may be subsidized by the seller and pegged very low (e.g., 1.9 percent from an automobile supplier) to stimulate sales; or they can be a source of profit (18 percent or more per year).

Typically, cash payment discounts, which range from 2 to 10 percent, are offered if payment is received within a specified number of days prior to the actual due date (paid in 10 days versus 30). Obviously, such discounts are intended to induce customers to pay quickly.

If a bill remains unpaid after a certain number of days (30, 60, 90, or more, depending on the vendor), interest charges usually accrue. However, businesses may be reluctant to impose interest charges, especially on their best customers, for fear of alienating them. A rule of thumb: if you impose interest charges, then collect them; if you don't, your collection policies all become a joke.

Companies with easy credit terms and simple credit applications may attract customers who perceive these conveniences as "friendliness." For example, Mobil Corporation—now Exxon Mobil Corporation—created its extremely convenient Speedpass to allow people to pay for their gas and other merchandise by waving a key chain fob in front of a pump.

Ideally, inventories exist in a state of barely controlled tension in which the manufacturer struggles to keep up with sales. While this tension indicates a healthy organization, an overcapacity with which salespeople can't keep pace is unhealthy.

The more frequently inventory turns over, the more money a business makes. But if the turns become too rapid, it may mean that the stock is running out. That many frustrated customers will cancel orders is one of the biggest risks of cutting inventory too fine.

Customers' tolerance levels vary according to the demand or nature of the business. For example, if Amazon.com, Inc., doesn't have the requested book, it will probably lose the order, because most likely the customer can locate it at the nearest Barnes & Noble, Inc., superstore and avoid shipping charges as well. So, it is vital to have enough inventory to fill nearly all, if not all, orders. On the other hand, people who order designer furniture understand they have to wait and are willing to do so. The point is that for every industry there is an optimal level of inventory that must be maintained in order to keep customers from turning away.

Inventories, as we noted earlier, are composed of raw materials, works-in-progress, and finished goods. Raw material inventory is channeled into the production process to maintain works-in-progress as well as a smoothly operating factory; the finished goods are what meet customer demand and also provide a safety stock of items.

Too little inventory can slow production or curb services; too much ties up assets unnecessarily. Service businesses also hold inventories, which include computer resources and skilled people. With rare exception, a growing company will need more inventory, a shrinking business, less. Reducing the size of a business during a crisis can be a good idea, because it allows unprofitable accounts to be dropped and raises cash by reducing inventories and receivables.

Businesses that experience seasonal cycles need to adjust their inventories accordingly. Accumulating materials several weeks or months ahead of the expected seasonal sales surge is one way to do that. Failure to understand seasonal fluctuations leads to product shortages first, then to their excess. Though surplus inventory can be liquidated for cash, it will have to be offered at a substantial discount if the enterprise is unloading overstock from the previous season. The corporate controller must find the right balance between avoiding superfluous purchases and accommodating real customer needs.

Industries prone to rapid change in taste or development, such as entertainment, fashion, and computer equipment, risk holding obsolete inventories if the value of their products or services falls precipitously within weeks or months of production. To limit this risk, publishers systematically drop most books from their catalogs shortly after publication; fashion houses quickly move designs from retail shops to discount stores; and computer manufacturers imitate Dell Computer Corporation's innovation—assembling every machine according to each customer's specifications, thus keeping finished-good inventories low. The disadvantage of inventory-reducing tactics, is that if carried to excess, sales from consumers who need or want their products right away will be lost.

When you aggressively reduce your inventory, you become more vulnerable to your vendors' problems. For example, a fire in an Asian chip factory disrupted Dell's production schedule as well as that of its competitors. But most companies gladly trade the risk of losing sales for the gains in working capital that are created by moving to JIT inventories and lean production.

Just-in-time inventory is arguably one of the most important management innovations of the twentieth century. The concept uses information technology to create a series of links: It connects the supplier with the producer, and the producer with the retailer in a continuous loop. The result is that new inventory is automatically delivered wherever it is needed.

Industries with declining product prices, such as computer assemblers, report accounting losses when their inventory values fall. When companies expect prices to fall for some reason (new competitors, production innovations, changing tastes), they should reduce inventories to their lowest possible permanent level. Permanent inventories are items that are never sold and serve only for display or demonstration purposes. Impermanent inventory, as the name implies, is the type that is intended to move.

Fear of declining prices motivates businesses to control the levels in both inventory categories. Improved order and delivery systems help to offset the adverse effects of reduced impermanent inventory on the customer—JIT inventory is an example of an ingenious improvement in that process.

Everyone benefits from such a smoothly functioning system. The producer maintains virtually no inventory, operates from a smaller facility, and is better informed about what is happening on the factory floor. Likewise, retailers hold limited inventories that are replenished whenever sales occur.

The proportionate breakdown of inventories into raw material, works-in-progress, and finished goods affects the size of the organization's physical operations and the speed with which products are put on shelves. These proportions also influence the amount of money invested in total inventories. Shifting the inventory split toward finished products reduces plant size and accelerates delivery times, but it also reduces flexibility. Holding more raw materials allows a wider range of products to be built but dramatically increases inventory. The controller must constantly monitor inventory levels to make sure they are serving the company as a whole, not just lightening the load of the manufacturing department.

Other factors affecting inventory levels include the number of outlets selling the product, the introduction of new products, and the constraints that the production process imposes. The paper industry is a good example of how processes increase inventories. Paper production begins with turning huge inventories of raw timber into piles of bark, wood chips, and wood pulp, some of which is sold as is; the rest is broken down further and converted into bulk paper. Businesses in this industry, such as the International Paper Company and Boise Cascade Corporation, manage inventory by balancing it with the varied needs of consumers in diverse product markets.

To some extent, inventory levels are preordained and not subject to managerial control. Even so, radical approaches can cut through obstacles and dramatically correct long-standing patterns of inventory imbalance. One such approach is to outsource inventory management, or even to outsource production itself. Though the loss of hands-on control provokes anxiety in some managers, we tend to recommend outsourcing because, in our experience, it is often the solution to stubborn inventory problems.

Moreover, we believe that almost any alternative is preferable to liquidating inventory. In our view, liquidation is always sad. The company is literally dumping its value in a desperate attempt to obtain working capital from its last remaining tangible assets.

Current Liabilities

Notes payable are written notices to pay a certain amount of money at a certain time. Offered by banks and some vendors, they are a form of short-term debt. They give a company a quick infusion of funds in the amount needed;

a disadvantage is that they require refinancing every year. Virtually all debt instruments, but especially short-term ones, demand regular interest payments and eventually a repayment of principal.

Few organizations can resist the lender's temptations, and many wind up with too much debt. Unfortunately, banks encourage over-borrowing by compensating their loan officers for the amount of new business they generate, instead of the number of healthy loans they arrange.

A good way to calculate the debt an enterprise can safely hold is to consider the two payment obligations: interest and principal. A business should expect to earn enough operating profit so that it can meet at least double its interest obligations. With this extra cushion, interest can be paid even if earnings unexpectedly drop by 50 percent. Since lending institutions usually insist on the right to demand loan repayment with only slight warning, a company that owes more short-term debt than money it can raise relatively quickly is skating on thin ice. Monies used to repay debts can come from "superfluous" inventories, funds held as cash, marketable securities, and cash flow from a single month of operations. If an organization thinks it needs a line of credit greater than what has been calculated as its prudent short-term debt level, then it should seriously consider whether its ambitions are worth the risks involved.

Working capital renewal usually begins with short-term loans from banks and vendors. Too often the amounts borrowed are excessive. To avoid over borrowing, you can match the maturity dates of your company's assets and liabilities. If 20 percent of assets are current (liquid), for example, then no more than 20 percent of liabilities should also be current. If the bulk of a company's assets are long term, then an equal share of its liabilities should be long-term obligations.

Accounts payable is the accountant's term for the money you owe vendors for purchases you have made. Although you should try to pay these bills within the time frame specified by the vendor, there is no reason to pay them early—with one important exception. Companies with adequate cash holdings should take advantage of cash discounts that vendors offer. The return on the use of that cash can equal nearly 40 percent per annum when the discount gives a 2 percent cut on invoices that are paid within 10 days instead of 30; this return probably exceeds the profitability of the basic operating business.

Items purchased with credit must be paid within a specific time frame, usually 30 or 60 days, though 90 days is possible. If you miss the cash discount period, we don't advise paying any sooner than necessary. While vendors expect to be paid by the end of the grace period, they may not assess late penalties if more time is needed, especially if you are considered a good customer.

Still, we don't recommend dragging out payments to vendors; you risk losing their cooperation at a later time when you urgently need their help with, say, a rushed shipment or a warranty service. Furthermore, vendors communicate among themselves, so whatever you gain from a little extra time to pay may be lost if you earn a bad reputation.

Organizations engaged in Phoenix Effect efforts usually encounter three accounts-payable issues: They fail to use cash discounts; they pay their bills too early; and they pay their bills too late. The controller must know the disposition of all three at all times. The only excuse for not taking a generous cash discount is that money is unavailable. It even makes sense to use a bank line that charges several points over the prime interest rate to obtain a cash discount that generates a 40 percent return on the invested money.

Making the mistake of paying bills either too soon or too late is often a consequence of poor accounting controls. Reasonably priced high-precision accounting software that allows all invoices to be logged and scheduled for payment is available. For accounts payable, software programs can match invoices to purchase orders, preventing you from paying an old, already-paid invoice or a fraudulent one.

Coordinating Assets and Liabilities

The adept management of working capital is critical for any company seeking the Phoenix Effect. It reflects the organization's ability to pay its bills and resolve financial issues with customers and creditors. We believe three basic rules govern doing this successfully.

- First, don't let the fact that you may not enjoy it interfere with your ability to perform it. Failing to manage your working capital professionally places the entire enterprise at risk. If neither you nor anyone else internally has the capability, go outside. Accounting functions are readily outsourced to competent individuals. Efforts to economize by having untrained personnel do the work are totally and always misguided.

- Second, conserve cash by never spending it impulsively; deliberate before paying money out and demand that your customers pay you in cash. Lean inventories, limited accounts receivable, and ample accounts payable all help to maintain a strong cash position. A company should be open to considering virtually anything that can speed inflow and slow outflow. Cash has a "them that has gets" effect: Banks are happy to make loans to a cash-rich organization; they balk at lending to a cash-poor company. Keeping a healthy cash flow at all times is the only solution.

- Third, always keep current assets and current liabilities in healthy proportion to each other. Ideally, current assets should exceed current liabilities by a margin ranging from 25 to 100 percent. Assets should surpass liabilities by a higher percentage if the inventories or the accounts receivable are old. Prior experience helps to quantify the necessary surplus for a particular organization.

Every enterprise is, of course, unique. How one company interprets and applies these three rules will be a little different from how every other organization does. But there can be no quarreling with the overarching principle: Managing working capital is vital and must be a part of any Phoenix Effect effort.

As we said at the outset, working-capital crises result from previous errors, which are avoidable if you follow the rules we have just discussed. And unless your company has suffered a mortal wound, these rules can save it from a capital crisis and restore its capital health.

CHAPTER 7

Get the Most from Employees

As a general rule, conscientious people make good products. But sometimes those same people lose their edge and start, unwittingly, to make inferior products. What happens then?

We want you to think about that question long before it comes up; even if it is one that you never encounter. In this chapter, we confront the realities of the human factor in business. We thoroughly examine the quandaries that seem inevitably to beset most organizations and their leaders when they try to reconcile people and profit. We want to help you derive the strongest contribution from your employees that is consistent with your bottom line, while, at the same time, respecting the fact that each is an individual.

First, we believe that all employees are vital, whatever jobs they perform, but those who deal with customers are every company's first line of offense and defense. While it is possible for a charming salesperson to sell a mediocre product, it is impossible for an offensive one to sell even a great product. If customers dislike your people, it won't be long before they dislike your products and take their business elsewhere.

Let's think about your defense first. If you have a product that isn't performing as well as expected, you anticipate complaints. In such a situation, who is your first line of defense? Obviously, it is an employee who answers the phone and speaks with the customer courteously, patiently, and helpfully (without promising any corrective steps that the organization has not yet agreed to).

You know that the business of business is making money; what you may not realize is how simple that business is. You need two fundamental ingredients—a good product that customers want to own and bright, charismatic people who will both sell it and, if necessary, defend it. And of the two—desired product and competent people—we believe that, in the long run, good people are more important than good products.

Just as the most talented oddsmaker should not expect to win every horse race that he or she bets on, you can't expect to produce one popular product after another. You can, however, cover your bets by staffing your enterprise with superb employees who will continue to reflect the company's strengths even when the products are weak.

It is your responsibility to keep those employees performing as well as they can. They won't remain superb without reliable leadership, and in fact, there is a perfect time to address this issue. Most successful companies have a defining moment when profits are skyrocketing, and business could not be better. That is precisely the time to look closely at your customer service. That you are earning more money than ever before indicates your product is terrific, but it doesn't necessarily mean the same about your customer service. It is the ideal time to examine your reputation and expand the success you are earning from your product to include customer service.

Every business wants to be known for its customer service. Although even a slow-but-steady giant such as Radio Shack Corporation will often come up with a hot product, it is its customer service that keeps it in business, year after year. There are trendier companies selling sexier products, but those products come and go. Radio Shack's ability to sustain itself is attributable to good customer service.

But the reality is this: While employees are clearly your company's most valuable resource, they are also one of your most controllable costs. This means that, if necessary, you must reduce those costs.

Employee expenses can be restrained by attrition: When people retire or resign, you hire only as many or as few people as are needed. But some economic conditions develop so fast that attrition alone can't address them. At those times, you confront the very unpleasant task of social engineering—a reduction in force, or RIF.

One of the reasons that a RIF is so traumatic is that business, as a whole, no longer views employees as mere workers. A major effort to raise the consciousness of the corporate world in recent years has helped business owners and executives regard their employees as "human capital." This change acknowledges how vital employees are to your organization. Moreover, it makes them less vulnerable to being fired suddenly. It is much harder to hand a pink slip to a person.

The term *human capital* elevates people to the level of capital assets, such as plants and equipment. It implies that people deserve at least as much attention and care as, say, your information technology equipment. If you neglect your employees and ignore their needs, they will break down in some way, too, or at least become less efficient, and eventually this is going to show up in your company's bottom line.

In essence, employers and employees need each other to succeed. Three tacit rules have evolved around that premise that define the relationships between them:

- The *exchange rule* means that the company pays a fair market wage in exchange for the employee's sincere work effort.

- The *ethical rule* says that both parties behave reasonably and show mutual respect.

- The *environmental rule* stipulates that companies provide a safe workplace that is free of danger and harassment.

Although these rules aren't statutory and are, in fact, rarely explicitly stated either publicly or privately, they are broadly accepted. Employees' jobs are at stake if they violate the rules; employers risk losing the employees, being sued, and having their workplace poisoned by acrimony. In the best of cases, if someone disrespects the rules, the employer and employee will analyze the incident together and use it as an opportunity to bring about constructive change.

Critical to the success of any Phoenix Effect process is that you observe the spirit as well as the letter of the rules.

Perhaps the greatest concern lies in how the exchange rule is interpreted and applied. Some employees mistrust any compensation scheme that isn't paid in wages and consider it a violation of the exchange rule. Yet Phoenix Effect plans often rearrange compensation packages to introduce incentives for meeting or exceeding goals. Doing so links an employee's total compensation to his or her work effort and performance. In the context of the Phoenix Effect, incentives motivate workers to focus their attention on strategic objectives. At the same time, they communicate a sense of urgency to the undertaking and may also reduce costs.

Clearly, fairness calls for both employee and employer to honor the three employment rules; and the Phoenix Effect promotes bilateral evaluation of them. Not surprisingly, employers and employees differ in their interpretations of the rules, especially the ones relating to environmental and ethical issues.

Of course, neither party should be the only one keeping the bargain. Though courts of law ensure that workers receive promised wages and benefits, they can do little when workers give less than an honest effort in exchange. The Phoenix Effect restructures worker-employer relationships so that both parties are penalized if they break their promises.

During a crisis that threatens to put a company out of business, it isn't uncommon to deviate from the rules. Emergency measures may require canceling or reducing planned wage and benefit increases, discharging all but essential workers, converting some employees from full time to part time, and outsourcing activities, or even whole divisions. Of course, such draconian measures are permissible only in very severe situations.

When the mission is to improve the company—as in a turnaround or transformation—ignoring the rules is ill-advised. Doing so imposes unnecessary emotional burdens on an already-distressed workforce; and this, in turn, jeopardizes cost savings and productivity gains.

The transitions required in any Phoenix Effect effort are difficult, and perhaps impossible, without the cooperation and support of employees. How then can you gain their cooperation? Two theories explain this psychological question, each suggesting a different way to motivate human behavior. One is called the *bountiful model* and the other, the *energetic model*.

The bountiful model posits that if you provide workers with excellent wages and benefits, you can safely expect them to do the right thing for the company. However, most companies that subscribe to it are performing well already. Would the bountiful model continue as their choice if their profits were lower and they had to take a hard look at employee costs?

The energetic model argues that if you always do what is demonstrably in the organization's best interest, employees will follow. That is, by crafting optimistic plans, strong leaders will motivate the workforce to respond energetically.

Both models, the bountiful and the energetic, can be applied at any Phoenix Effect stage, but how do you know which is better? Even casual observation reveals a number of unsuccessful companies with contented workers as well as successful businesses with unhappy workers. This raises the possibility that an environment oriented toward employees is neither necessary nor sufficient for corporate success.

If the workers' contentment isn't a prerequisite for an enterprise's success, an alternative is to focus on the necessity of an attractive pay package. The idea here is to create a system in which compensation and performance are inseparable and hard work and loyalty are rewarded. Workers receiving salary bonuses, stock options, or special gifts as incentives may or may not be content, but if the system has been well designed, they are, most assuredly, being fairly paid (meeting the exchange rule) and are working at their peak level (meeting the ethical rule). In other words, some workers value material rewards more highly than they do feeling content at work.

These conclusions don't alter the fact that people are the first priority in any Phoenix Effect effort; that increasing employees' productivity is the principal objective of the people review stage of the Phoenix Effect remains true, too. The pragmatic approach rules. If the company's profits go up because people are content, then having gratified employees is crucial. Likewise, if keeping workers satisfied doesn't demonstrably promote higher productivity, then other human resource stratagems should take precedence.

The money spent to improve the condition of workers— enriched benefits, comfortable ambiance, the opportunity for individual empowerment—comes from the common pool of corporate funds. Personnel issues that are resolvable with little or no cost should certainly be undertaken immediately.

However, a costly personnel initiative must compete with all other company options and convince management that it will exceed the returns of any of them. Only then will it receive an allocation from the corporate investment pool, which provides funding for the organization's three other main areas of investment: physical plant, manufacturing processes, and product development and sales.

In reality, it is likely that you will have to ration your investments in human resources; doing so may be the only way to make sure that the funds aren't exploited for purposes that won't benefit the company.

Even though establishing and enhancing human capital requires resources for which several other major areas of the corporation are competing, we argue that people are the organization's primary resource. After all, without them, business stops.

Thus, to keep workers satisfied and motivated, businesses seek a delicate balance that, on the one hand, gives employees what they want and, on the other, does so without threatening the organization's cost effectiveness. Frank conversations between employers and employees can reveal problems about the job or inadequacies in the workplace that may be obvious only to current employees and wouldn't surface any other way. Addressing an employee issue may simultaneously eliminate related product, plant, or process issues.

The Employee Audit

An employee audit is an early step in the Phoenix Effect process and is designed to help companies deal effectively with people. Like an accounting audit, the objectives of a personnel audit are to measure the balance between the assets and liabilities of the organization's human resources and to identify any recent gains and losses in that area.

People assets include the supply, productivity, and intellectual capital of workers. Their aggregate value is related to skill and demographic factors such as a worker's age, training, and location. Liabilities include wage and benefit packages, pensions, union membership, rate of employee turnover, workplace sabotage, and employee injuries.

The difference between human resource assets and their liabilities is referred to as *labor force net worth*. This concept is parallel to the notion of economic value added, which is the difference between the revenues a product yields and its total incurred costs. It is also similar to Karl Marx's concept of surplus labor value.

Human resource gains and losses reflect what progress was made during the year on people issues. This results-oriented evaluation describes changes in asset and liability values. For example, a report might indicate that fewer workers were employed but those few produced more output. It might reveal that these workers earned more money in the aggregate than did their predecessors. Other updated data would include a report on the changes, if any, in the number of workers injured, how many defective products were produced by which shift at what plant, and the number of workers who left their jobs.

The audit investigates the status of a company's human resources, then guides the organization toward an appropriate plan of action that will address its findings. The audit aims to increase productivity and move the corporation closer to fulfilling its mission.

People audits are almost never part of a Phoenix Effect plan if the business is in crisis. At that time, it may be useful to answer some straightforward questions, say about compensation or the employee mix. But most, if not all, of the employee audit belongs in turnaround or transformation assignments.

We believe that the employee audit is a powerful tool for renewal. Yet we also know that companies can resist untried ideas. Therefore, we suggest testing the audit in various departments to distinguish aspects more or less suited to your needs, before involving the whole organization. That way, you can learn a lot while risking little. Like other steps in the Phoenix Effect process, the wisest course is to introduce and implement the audit gradually.

Phoenix Effect specialists use the employee audit because it gives them data that show how specific aspects of the employment relationship can work to improve the enterprise's profitability. Obviously, a Phoenix Effect plan can't be conceived before the team is thoroughly familiar with both how the business operates and what precisely is expected of workers. While audits can uncover several problems for which there are solutions—unbalanced workforces, inappropriate compensation packages, and technological training deficits are examples—the impeding issues at any particular company must also be identified. Answering the following questions can help uncover underlying obstacles: Is the right number of workers employed? Are compensation levels suitable? Are workers divided among the facilities correctly? Have employees been properly trained? Do workers have sufficient incentives to want to reduce the incidence of defects, sabotages, and departures?

Managers need to consider problems from both short- and long-term perspectives, and decide when one or the other view will lead to more productivity. A problem about compensation levels, for instance, is usually amenable to short-term modification, while, say, training deficits require a longer-term solution. Enacting changes over a prolonged period of time—attending productivity-enhancing classes, for example—helps managers understand and appreciate the need for the transition. In addition, gradual change affords the organization an opportunity to assess progress at various stages.

Ironically, the outcome of the people review may prompt the company to downsize. Just as there are disagreements among accountants and managers when the accountants complete a corporate audit, there will be disagreements over the results of an employee audit. The key to reducing a workforce successfully is to retain the best workers, dismiss the worst, and in the end, have the correct number of employees. Though it sounds like a simple idea, it is bedeviled by two difficulties: identifying the best employees, then unseating the rest.

The fact that the enterprise's ideal size is yet to be determined further hinders the process. Thus, for example, if problems continue to mount after you have reduced the workforce, it indicates that either you didn't reduce sufficiently to meet current demands or the reduction wasn't the problem in the first place. But that doesn't justify deeper cuts, which would be harmful if business rebounds.

The audit begins with an in-depth review of the company and its workers. Ideally, it is timed to coincide with salary reviews, when managers presumably have the relevant information on hand. The data can be benchmarked against the organization's figures from past audits as well as against whatever information on competitors can be procured from public documents. This will help determine if you have overvalued human assets and underfunded human liabilities.

An annual human resource audit helps uncover problems related to people and also recommends ways to fix them. It draws attention to issues before they become impediments and can promote communication and efficiency. Managers, union representatives, and individual workers all participate.

Obviously, a company that continues its preaudit pattern of lower sales per employee or higher compensation costs, when compared with its competitors, isn't benefiting from what was discovered in its audit. Organizations that ignore their workers provide a breeding ground for trouble; perhaps the most destructive result is the needless waste of an opportunity to improve productivity.

Incentives

People expend immense effort trying to win prizes—a human trait that managers keep in mind when they design compensation packages that aim to invigorate productivity, generate ideas, and encourage cooperation.

Needless to say, ill-conceived incentive systems can produce unexpected and even disastrous results. Be sure to scrutinize any new compensation plan before adopting it to make sure that no counterproductive incentive has been inadvertently included. Some typical mistakes include rewarding current or short-term activities rather than long-term ones; rewarding the amount of new sales rather than the amount of profit; and defining the reward so narrowly that once a prearranged goal is reached, motivation evaporates. An effective incentive system encourages employees to cooperate, establish reasonable goals, and target long-term objectives, such as stock price or net earnings after all expenses.

The only criterion that should be applied to an incentive plan is whether or not it works. It doesn't have to be elaborate or expensive to fund. A case in point is Tricon Global Restaurants, Inc.

In late 1997, PepsiCo, Inc., spun off its restaurant businesses, Taco Bell, Pizza Hut, and Kentucky Fried Chicken (KFC), and formed Tricon. Though it appeared to be a formidable enterprise, in fact, it had serious problems, including enormous debt, some not-so-profitable restaurants, and a labor turnover rate that exceeded 150 percent per year. Tricon battled these problems head on.

Incentives were the weapon chosen to attack the turnover rate, which was costing the business $800 each time a worker had to be replaced. To encourage job loyalty, Tricon created employee teams that were rewarded when their restaurants met high standards for service and cleanliness. Though quite modest in actual value (about $100 per team), the rewards created work units composed of employees who, it turned out, tended to bond and become very supportive of each other. Preliminary results showed a 50 percent reduction in turnover rates. Store managers, who also joined the teams, were given $20,000 in stock options with additional shares offered to people who performed particularly well.

The success of Tricon's incentives was reflected on Wall Street. On March 29, 1999, when the Dow Jones Industrial Average first hit 10,000, Tricon's stock reached $70 per share, up from its initial public offering price of $31 in late 1997.

Although, it will appear at first glance that the next organization we study, the Edison Schools, Inc., has nothing in common with Tricon, it does in fact resemble it in two ways. A large portion of the consumers of both are teenagers, and like Tricon, Edison has an incentive program that really works. Dedicated to improving public education and currently operating more than 136 schools from California to Massachusetts, the Edison is a for-profit enterprise. As such, it can provide teachers, to whom the fewest incentives are rendered, a virtually unheard-of opportunity. It offers them stock options.

Edison's founder, Christopher Whittle, plans to expand the company to more than a thousand schools, but to do so he needs evidence that Edison students are, in fact, getting a superior education. Clearly, this calls for hard work and extraordinary dedication on the part of Edison's teachers. Their incentive, Whittle believes, is the stock option plan he has devised, which yokes the interests of his business with those of the teachers.

Still, it is clear that the methods by which standardized state tests are instituted and corrected require scrupulous, ongoing monitoring, but, as recent news reports of a Dallas, Texas, teacher who corrected state testing results indicate, careful monitoring is necessary to avoid overzealous Edison instructors.

If you take the concept of incentives seriously, institute a company policy wherein a direct supervisor meets privately with his or her employees once a month, if not more frequently, so that employees can receive ongoing feedback systematically. We suggest that you let this process replace the annual review, which we sum up as an awkward 15-minute conversation with an employee you have barely spoken with for a year, in which you tell him or her the status of his or her work performance for the past 12 months. It has little, if any, value.

If you are the boss, arrange for your office to send out notes that praise employees when they win something—a promotion, a contract, a new client. If the accomplishment is extraordinary, send a handwritten note to the person's home. But, make sure you don't overdo it, which will make it less special. Only praise an accomplishment when that praise can be generous, timely, and genuine.

Furthermore, never miss an opportunity to strengthen the bonds among your best people. For instance, if a supervisor tells you about an employee's superior work, tell the employee that her supervisor did so. It will help her trust her supervisor. On his part, the supervisor appreciates that you mentioned his name, and he now knows that you recognize his valuable role in developing the human capital in his group. And you have won the gratitude of both of them.

Cooperation

In addition to incentives, the Phoenix Effect encourages workers' performances by supporting their needs, while at the same time encouraging them to understand and support the organization's aims. But how far should a company go to please its workers?

Businesses answer this question differently, but all make decisions about the costs and benefits of cooperating with employees. Paying very little attention to workers may cause them to feel alienated and disenfranchised, but doing so may save money. Offering too much attention may create an unmotivated workforce, but it might help to promote loyalty.

Cooperation takes many forms. Workers should feel free to contribute their ideas if they think they can improve efficiency or sales efforts. Often, when employees feel empowered, they can help resolve problems quickly, which increases customer satisfaction. Cooperation among workers and management has the potential to make the workplace a pleasant and comfortable environment, which is conducive to achieving corporate goals. The following account of two companies in the same industry that have taken different approaches to cooperation illustrates the complexity of the issues involved.

In key ways, Delta Air Lines, Inc., and America West Holdings Corporation represent opposite sides of the airline business. Delta is a successful carrier and dominant in many markets. America West is far smaller, and, in 1994, it emerged from bankruptcy court as a new company. Both operate in similar oligopolistic, but geographically diverse, environments. Delta's flights are concentrated in the eastern United States; America West flies mainly in the West.

Historically, both airlines have had excellent working relationships with employees. America West, for example, was known as a place where people loved to work. Delta's protective attitude toward its employees took a turn for the worse in 1993 and 1994 when its financial fortunes sank. To reverse course and boost productivity, it cut back on its number of employees, then imposed a 2 percent pay cut on those who remained. America West, confronting a crisis more severe than Delta's, in fact, struggling to climb out of bankruptcy, went even further in this direction. It cut wages and benefits so they were the lowest of any company in the airline industry.

The consequences were predictable: The financial situations of both airlines improved, but labor relations suffered. Delta bounced back from its adversity, and during its 1998 contract negotiations with its pilots, offered to raise their base salary to $171,000 per year, nearly 5 percent above that of pilots at AMR Corporation's American Airlines, a close competitor. In 1999, Delta's earnings were more than $1 billion.

America West also began making money again, and in 1998 it achieved record profits. This company, too, made generous salary offers during its 1999 contract negotiations that would move its employees closer to the mean wages and benefits for the industry.

But in their quests for recovery, both airlines lost favor with their employees. America West's new chief executive, William Franke, alienated employees by firing mechanics and outsourcing their work, suing flight attendants (unsuccessfully) to stop them from unionizing, and reducing salaries and benefits for the airline's bottom rung of workers. Though Franke continued at the helm of America West after the bankruptcy, Delta replaced Ronald Allen, the author of its austerity plan, with Leo Mullins, whose reputation as a "people person" was well suited for this company's roiled labor relations.

Following their financial recoveries, both airlines offered favorable wage and benefit packages, but their positions on cooperating with workers diverged. America West's attitude was less than conciliatory. When the union threatened to strike unless management improved wages and benefits, Franke said, "As much as we want to reach an agreement, we will not compromise the viability of the company to do so" (Scott McCartney, "America West Con-

tract War Is over More Than Money," *Wall Street Journal,*
March 8, 1999).

Delta's tone was different. Though pilots threatened to
withhold approval of the contract offer, it wasn't because
they were dissatisfied with the terms. The pilots were
upset because, in their view, Mullins had not included
them in the management of the organization as much as
he should have. Mullins, in response, proposed to return
to the previous closer relationship that management and
employees had shared, but he rejected the latter's request
for a seat on the board. Delta's well-paid workers were able
to put issues unrelated to money at the forefront, while
America West's could not. Bending a bit on the employees'
demand for more cooperation, Delta continues to prosper; America West, which didn't budge on this issue, still
is in search of a better day.

Handling Big Layoffs

There are numerous theories on how and when to conduct layoffs. We offer here a distillation of what we have
learned from our experiences from counseling hundreds
of chief executives through one of senior management's
most painful tasks.

The first step is to decide who you will let go. Take your
time; investigate this thoroughly and be absolutely sure
that you have identified the right employees. Proceed
cautiously; don't decide on Monday who to lay off on
Wednesday.

As it is being compiled, the list of names must be the
company's most closely guarded secret. Once you have
assembled it, move as fast as possible. Odds are that peo-

ple sense that layoffs are coming and, of course, are anxious to know if they will be affected.

Next, with the counsel of the fewest possible trusted advisers and lieutenants, define how the official objectives of the layoff will be presented. As a rule, we suggest that you couch them in very neutral, impersonal language.

For example, focus on cutting payroll, not people. Push down to department heads the need for an X percent reduction in payroll. And make this nonnegotiable, because you are about to perform one of an executive's hardest jobs—a task so unpleasant and results so unattainable that some companies will hire consultants to do it for them.

Announce the specific percentage by which you have to cut payroll. In so doing, you have set a definite goal that must be achieved. Clarify that, unfortunately, this reduction can't be accomplished through any other cost-saving measure. Otherwise, people will offer to stop ordering supplies and deducting lunch from petty cash, which will make the situation more painful for everyone.

Your aim is to create a mind-set in which the layoffs are necessitated by the need to raise your gross margin level. If you say that you want "30 heads out of here," you undermine the relationships among middle managers and their employees.

It is essential that you establish a consistent plan for employees' severance packages. Determine what is standard in your industry or what your company has done in the past, then don't waver from it. So, if your organization settles on, say, one week of pay for each year of service, that is the arrangement you will offer to everyone, and it is the only arrangement. If your severance packages vary, you are likely to find yourself facing (and losing) lawsuits. The same applies to benefits. Implying that the severance terms are negotiable, now or in the future, will work to everyone's disadvantage.

We advise you to have professional grief counselors on the premises the day of the layoffs. One scenario that we suggest is this: When an employee leaves the termination interview, he or she is taken directly to another office, where a counselor is ready to talk about any and every aspect of the employee's future. Writing a new resume and seeking new employment are just a few examples. That the counselor is ready to talk to the employee doesn't mean that the reverse is true. In most cases, the grief counselors will either make themselves available or offer a referral to another professional if the employee can't yet express his or her feelings but may want to later. By no means should there be any link between the grief counselor and the person who laid off the employee. The bifurcation ought to be pronounced. Whenever possible, involve a third person to retrieve the individual's computer, pass code, company credit cards, and anything else that belongs to the company. It is unnecessarily demeaning for the person who is taking your job away to also ask you literally to empty your pockets.

Your next responsibility is to set the time frame.

Contrary to a lot of other advice you may receive, we recommend that layoffs be conducted on a Monday morning. Though Friday is often the chosen day, we believe strongly that is a mistake. Let us explain why we strongly favor Mondays.

Needless to say, when people are laid off, they are upset and agitated. And since it is difficult, if not impossible, to commence a job search over a weekend, you are leaving your former employee with two full days of unstructured time. One way of dealing with being laid off is to immerse yourself in a new project, which for most will begin with looking for work, perhaps networking to learn what positions are available. You don't want to inadvertently take that option away. Furthermore, it is unfair of the company to enact such a traumatic event without giving the remaining employees an opportunity to ask questions and process the changes. They, too, will be worried and unsettled all weekend, which brings us to your final task in this process.

To begin damage control, you should plan ahead and call a meeting for all remaining employees to take place late Monday afternoon. This is where you will present the financial data explaining why the layoffs were necessary and how the saved costs will help put the company back on course. We suggest you describe the measures you took to protect those who were let go—that is, the generous severance packages and the counselors and outplacement services you have made available. You want the people who are staying to believe that their friends and coworkers were treated as well as possible given the company's financial problems.

Unfortunately, some organizations have made a horrible mess of laying people off, and no doubt others will bungle the process in the future. These situations are awful, sometimes traumatic, even when they go exactly as they were planned. We have one case example of a badly botched lay-off plan.

Oklahoma Tire and Supply Company (OTASCO), as we mentioned earlier, claimed to be selling tires and appliances, but in fact, it was really selling credit. Every item in the store had a sign that announced the payment amount—$35 per month for this washer; $29 per month for that dryer—but no actual price signs. If you wanted a price, the salesperson had to look it up for you.

The company's fundamental problem was that its business model no longer worked. It had stopped making money from customers in two ways. In addition to charging close to full retail prices, it was making an extra profit by financing the cost at high rates. Customers realized that there was no reason to buy OTASCO's $500 washer when they could get the same one from a competitor, such as Sears, Roebuck & Company, for a little more than $400 and charge the total cost to their Visa cards.

When OTASCO finally ran out of cash, company officers decided to lay off 1,500 workers on a Friday. The following Monday, OTASCO found itself amidst chaos—besieged by all kinds of computer issues and payable and receivable issues, which caused the enterprise to come to a halt. Precisely what happened was never determined, but it seems clear that disgruntled employees or their friends tampered with the code and the payroll-processing keys. Perhaps in the disorganization that defined that Friday afternoon, people slipped out, and then back in, with their pass cards. Considerable assets and inventory galore were missing.

With better planning, OTASCO might have avoided the pillage. Because the layoffs were kept secret until the last possible minute on Friday, no facet of the infrastructure, such as security guards and human resource people, were asked to work later than the ordinary closing time of 5 p.m. When they finally were warned, it was too late for most to change their plans. Among the goods missing from OTASCO were pass cards, desktop computers, laptops, gasoline charge cards, and, of course, some inventory.

The problems didn't stop with material loss. On Monday, the remaining employees were circulating a petition that demanded a meeting with management to find out why the layoffs occurred. Workers were extremely upset, and, unsurprisingly, productivity fell to almost nothing through Wednesday. Though management finally decided to hold a conference call in order to calm the remaining stores throughout the United States, there was no plan beyond that. By now, five days of chaos and confusion had elapsed.

Mourning the loss of their colleagues, the remaining employees grew increasingly upset. When customers entered the store on Monday, Tuesday, and Wednesday, they were greeted by overtly unhappy and surly employees.

It was a human-capital fiasco from which the business never recovered. Many things were handled incorrectly: It had no uniform script of severance policies, and in fact, rumors circulated that some managers granted individuals extra severance pay because they felt sorry for them. Certain employees actually talked their managers out of letting them go, by arguing, "You have the wrong person. You didn't do your homework." And the managers backed down.

At every step, OTASCO is an example of how not to execute layoffs.

We advise you always to remember that in numerous surveys people have ranked losing their jobs as one of the top two causes of depression and distress, second only to divorce. Some people become suicidal: Those who have no family or support systems are particularly vulnerable. Individuals who have been at the company for a long time and can't imagine the future without it may also be more susceptible.

The point is, don't ever underestimate the importance of the separation meeting. Be thoroughly prepared, even have a script in front of you. Managers who are inexperienced or uncertain about their capacity to carry out this assignment should be trained in how to do it appropriately.

Remember, too, that your job is to tell the employee that he or she is no longer needed at the company, and to do so clearly, with finality, and leaving no room for negotiation. We suggest that you resist your temptation to offer comfort. If, for example, a terminated employee says, "I hear the XYZ division is still hiring; can I transfer over? Just consider me," don't succumb to your impulse to say, "Okay." You don't want to contradict your earlier, unambiguous message because, among other reasons, the employee's grief and healing process can't begin until he or she realizes that this job is over. It is wise to anticipate and be prepared for questions like this, including offers to stay on at a reduced salary. You should review other options at the company long before you meet with the employee. Your job is to clear the way for the next step in the employee's and the organization's lives.

This is the time for a fresh start—for employee and company alike.

CHAPTER 8

Get the Most from Products

Fred, Inc., had an identity crisis. It was trying to be a cross between Wal-Mart Stores, Inc., and Dollar General Corporation or a comparable cut-rate, small-town retailer.

When coauthor Carter Pate walked through his first Fred's store, he saw at once that the company was confused and was confusing its potential customers. Your image, he said, just doesn't add up. "Your stores aren't anywhere near the size of Wal-Mart. So if you're touting vast selection, you've disappointed customers on that score. Furthermore, your pricing model doesn't match your claim that Fred's is where families with a household family income of $15,000 should shop." He told the management straight out: "Neither you nor your customers really know what you are."

The solution to Fred's ambiguous identity was a realignment of the stores' product and pricing mix. If you want to alter and sharpen consumers' perceptions of who you are and what you offer, you may find that changing your product-price mix is often as effective as changing the products themselves. (Product-price mix, of course, is also a critical aspect of a company's orientation. See discussion of Sears, Roebuck & Company in Chapter 3.)

In the case of Fred's Super Dollar Stores, he recommended a two-tier pricing system, which required identifying the 100 to 200 best-selling items, pricing them to undercut all competition, and using them as loss leaders to lure people into the stores. Once there, we bet that customers would buy other items that had higher profit margins.

Fred's best-sellers were, quite predictably, commodities in categories that consumers buy regularly. They included bath soap (Dial), toilet tissue (Scott), paper towels (Bounty), laundry detergent (Tide), plus an assortment of popular goods in other categories, such as Juicy Fruit gum and WD-40. On these and dozens more top sellers, he persuaded Fred's stores to take 1 to 2 percent margins—or less—because he knew cost-conscious customers would quickly realize that they couldn't get better prices anywhere.

The plan intentionally cut across all product lines, appealing to people in different market segments in order to attract as many customers as possible. Then they continuously called attention to Fred's bargains with in-store signs and hand out pricing lists, newspaper ads, and mailbox stuffers. Promotion and advertising never strayed from the top 100 or so items that everyone needs each day—all available at Fred's stores at rock-bottom prices. Pricing didn't apply only to individual products, but to groupings of them as well.

With this system, you are in charge of your internal pricing model, which is important because you avoid the futile exercise of begging the Procter & Gamble Company or another customer-product manufacturer for a special deal that it won't even offer to Wal-Mart. When companies as large as P&G give you a deal, they do so based on the volume you move. But if you are buying soap for 32 cents per bar and selling it for 42 cents, consider selling it at 32 cents. The price will attract customers, who may buy other higher-margin items in that aisle.

Remember, however, creative pricing alone rarely carries the day. How products are placed is vital to the strategy. First, place your cut-rate merchandise throughout the store; don't concentrate these items in one section. Second, always place them either on the top or bottom shelf of the aisle. Market research has shown that consumers tend to purchase what they see at eye level. If you position your higher-margin products at the eye level of a person of average height and your low-margin goods above or below (making them harder to find), you encourage more profitable purchases.

Products and Strategy

Let's step back at this point and take a broad view of how and where products figure in any Phoenix Effect effort. (By "products" we mean both goods and services, except when referring specifically to services.)

A corporate strategy articulates how a company plans to achieve its Phoenix Effect goals and fulfill its mission. Examples of strategic objectives include raising market share, being the low-cost producer, or having the highest-quality product.

How goods are deployed is part of every corporate strategy. A successful product fits well with the strategy and is well received in the marketplace. For instance, an objective of the Ford Motor Company is to sell a quality car in every price range, but that requires a prerequisite strategy, which is to design the products to achieve that goal.

Managers decide the best way to offer something new so that it helps an organization realize its strategic objectives. Whether it is successful depends on the product team's skills, the resources at the team's disposal, and good fortune. As a rule, an organization should eliminate items that no longer serve strategic objectives; it can either sell them to other companies or discontinue them. Hasbro, Inc., one of the two largest toy manufacturers, actively manages its products, culling through them to identify winners.

Products fail for a host of reasons. The strategy behind them may be faulty, or a shrewd strategy may be poorly executed. Locating the problem is the first step in resuscitating one that is failing. A fault in its design is relatively easy to fix: Redo the design. Flaws in the underlying strategy are harder to uncover, especially when the investigator, as so often happens, is also the author of the strategy. Most of the time, mistakes in execution are blamed for product failures, but not always justly. In all cases, the problem must be identified, thoroughly and objectively investigated, then fixed accordingly.

To be useful, a strategy must be realistic and consistent with the organization's resources and competitive environment. Strategy development begins with an assessment by senior managers of a company's strengths and vulnerabilities. As they craft the strategy, managers consider numerous factors, such as technology, labor force, manufacturing and distribution resources and skills, owned patents, competition, imposed regulations, and funding. A strategy guides a company's scope, orientation, and scale, and it defines how products will be positioned, as well as how the organization will deal with those of competitors.

Strategies are impermanent. Unforeseen events compel managers to modify them so that they align with changing realities. A good manager is market driven, stays abreast of trends, keeps on top of customers' concerns, monitors competitors' activities, and knows how to use all this information to guide strategic adjustments. Changes in strategy refocus how products are sold and help the business target new market opportunities.

Strategic refocusing should be constant and unrelenting. For example, Home Depot, Inc., based in Atlanta, Georgia, has so dominated its market segment that there is little room for competitors to grow at rates anywhere near its historic average.

Yet even in robust times, Home Depot is busy renovating its business strategy. After extolling the virtues of doing it yourself for years, Home Depot is beginning to offer product installation services for extensive projects, such as vinyl siding and roofing. A new subsidiary offers complete kitchen and bathroom design and remodeling services. While these new services represent a change in scope, not to mention a dramatic expansion of product mix, they are clearly also strategic shifts, because they fundamentally modify the enterprise.

Home Depot's recharged strategy is likely to work for several reasons. First, consumers see Home Depot as a trustworthy, high-quality, and reasonably priced brand. (In our lexicon, it has the right orientation.) Second, Home Depot's competitors are individual craftspeople— a highly diverse assortment of entrepreneurs ranging from dedicated cabinetmakers to big home-remodeling contractors, and nearly everything in between. Third, Home Depot's managers and executives are detail oriented, customer friendly, and conscientious. Chances are good that with this idea, the organization will hit another home run.

Like Home Depot, McDonald's Corporation, based in Oak Brook, Illinois, wants to widen its focus and is seeking new strategic opportunities. The ubiquitous fast-food colossus owes its remarkable rise over the second half of the twentieth century, largely, to, America's (and now the world's) burger addiction. Today, the Golden Arches bestride the planet, while competing brands sizzle next door to just about every one, suggesting that the hamburger market may be close to overdone.

To avoid being left behind, McDonald's new chairman and chief executive officer, Jack M. Greenberg, is moving the company into the pizza, chicken, ice cream, and hotel businesses. The pizza facet of this strategic plan began with the purchase of a successful 143-restaurant chain, Donatos Pizzeria Corporation, which is as committed to high quality as McDonald's is to cleanliness and product uniformity. Donatos sells an "award-winning" pizza, which is significant since McDonald's earlier attempt to add pizza to its menu failed because of the pizza's poor quality. In most cases, the Donatos outlets will be physically separate from the McDonald's outlets, though some may be attached.

Chicken dinners joined McDonald's business menu when it bought 750 Boston Market restaurants out of bankruptcy court. Boston Market provides good locations and an appealing format, but the McDonald's touch is expected to increase volume. And Greenberg is adding ice cream in interesting combinations and new food bundles with the hope of attracting new consumers.

McDonald's has built two hotels in Switzerland, a bold expansion in scope that relies heavily on the company's existing brand to attract patrons. Success with the hotels would confirm that good managers tied to an appealing orientation can accomplish just about anything.

For Sun Country Airlines, based in Mendota Heights, Minnesota, strategic refocusing meant a switch in 1998 from flying only charters to providing scheduled passenger service. Sun Country's principal product, airline seats, hasn't changed; the shift is in how the seats are marketed and sold. With a corporate philosophy that puts its customers' needs ahead of the enterprise's costs, Sun Country describes itself as a "customer-first" airline (Kristin Miller, Sun Country's director of customer service, press release, December 15, 1999). In an era of apathetic seeming air carriers with sometimes unfriendly personnel, Sun Country attempts to offer something different.

By the time it was bought by new owners in 1997, the airline had become the nation's second largest charter carrier with more than 1,200 employees, a fleet of 15 jets, and annual sales in excess of $250 million. Sun Country's new management reviewed its strategic options and decided to transform the business into a scheduled passenger carrier. The timing seemed exactly right: Air carriers were earning their highest annual profits in the industry's history, and certain carriers dominated airport hubs to the point of having practically no competition. Sun Country's primary competitor, Northwest Airlines Corporation, provides nearly 90 percent of the flights out of both Detroit, Michigan, and Minneapolis, Minnesota. It is a lucrative market: On some full flights—for example, between Boston, Massachusetts, and Detroit—Northwest earns profits exceeding $15,000 on a cost of less than $5,000.

Sun Country hopes to undersell Northwest by 30 to 50 percent per passenger and will offer friendly service, as well. The young contender's success is predicated on three assumptions: First, that the 2.6 million customers who used Sun for charter flights in 1998 will use the carrier as a scheduled line now; second, that air travelers are price sensitive and will abandon Northwest for a lower-cost carrier; and third, that federal regulations will protect Sun against predatory pricing by big lines that could drive it out of business.

Successful Phoenix Effect strategies almost always begin with products that customers clearly need and want or that improve the quality of their lives, such as cheap, fast, comfortable air travel. Strategies that won't veer from their organization's core competencies and refuse to be influenced by popular products may miss the market entirely. Obviously, core competencies are very important, but even more vital is that your organization continuously develops and brings to market goods that actually fill consumers' current needs.

Though most strategic changes are incremental, some are necessary responses to financial crises or to sudden upheavals in a company's chief market. In such cases, time is of the essence, and strategy revisions rely heavily on changing your products quickly. With the luxury of time, a less hurried and more systematic strategic redesign would be part of a Phoenix Effect effort.

Product modification can take three different forms: cosmetic, expansive (i.e., moving along a product platform), or deletive.

Cosmetic changes alter external, easily adjusted characteristics, such as color, package size, or taste. They leave the basic item unchanged.

Expansive changes create newer models and related wares on the foundation, or platform, of an original product. The new item may be less expensive, possess more or different features, incorporate higher quality, or appeal to a niche market, but the key here is the use of an existing design, marketing plan, or technology.

There are three kinds of *deletive changes.* With total deletion, every vestige of a product is discontinued. In market-specific deletions, product distribution is condensed to fewer markets. The third kind is product line slenderizing, which reduces, but doesn't eliminate, the line.

What are the relative merits of cosmetic, expansive, and deletive changes? Let's examine each in turn.

Cosmetic Changes

Though easy to implement, cosmetic product alterations are least effective over the long run. They are too superficial to challenge competitors' new merchandise and too insignificant to cause profound changes in consumers' tastes.

Expansive or Product Platform Changes

These are the hardest, costliest switches to implement. They require new product-development efforts, including design engineering, marketing research, and prototype test-marketing. However, by enabling products to evolve and respond to market forces, they promise the most reliable long-term results.

In the automotive industry, the Ford Motor Company enlists feedback from customers to help it continually expand from its product platforms. The high cost of failure in that industry inhibits some manufacturers from releasing new products and leads them to imitate what has worked in the past. Ford, however, isn't skittish.

Aware that customers want cars that work both mechanically and aesthetically, Ford convenes panels of consumers to guide its design process. For example, three consumer task forces worked on the Ford Focus. Members of one team worked with their noses to ensure that the new vehicle had an appealing scent; the second drove the car to make sure that its look and feel were right; and the third tested the controls and knobs for appearance, comfort, and convenience.

The key to this effort's success was a change in Ford's culture: Engineers who were accustomed to deciding what customers "should" want had to step back and pay attention to what customers were actually stating. Ford allowed those recommendations to guide the changes it made to the new car as the product platform evolved.

Expanding from a product platform is an efficient way to grow. Compare Volkswagen AG's renaissance during the past decade with Nissan Motor Company, Ltd. Nissan maintains 25 platforms as the bases for its cars. Volkswagen has just four, from which it crafts a startling variety of automobiles. The same chassis carries the VW Beetle, Golf, and Jetta; the Audi A3 and TT Coupe; and the Skoda Octavia. When consumers look at them, they see six different cars, but in fact, they are all sitting on the same chassis. The German automaker saves costs with its efficiency and its relatively small inventory which Nissan's less flexible platforms cannot match.

Sony Corporation boasts a classic platforming success in the fabled Walkman and Discman, the lightweight musical appliances it pioneered. Sony perpetually updates its product offerings. The Discman evolved from a relatively simple machine to a bass-enhanced version to an ESP (electronic shock protector) version. One recent revolution is the Super Audio CD. Along the way, other models have added cosmetic changes, such as the sporty yellow outer cases.

The Super Audio machine, which costs nearly $4,000, uses "direct-stream digital" technology to replicate sound waves so that they are virtually identical to live music. Like most of the modifications made to Sony's original CD-product platform engine, the changes are real and profound. At each step in its product's evolution, consumers abandon the current technology to buy the better machine. Sony's new product introduction philosophy appears to be "if you build a better machine, consumers will buy it."

Significantly, Sony is one of the few corporations that can make this philosophy work. Many companies could have avoided building better machines that no one wanted if their strategists had adequately tested the market before production. Sony, on the other hand, has created better products so often that its brand alone captures customers for almost any new one.

Product Deletions

Like cosmetic changes, these can be implemented rather easily. Because they radically alter the product line composition, they may negatively affect the profitability of remaining products. Hence, they are risky and should be undertaken only after careful deliberation. Product deletions are a form of downsizing. They permit a company to shrink in an orderly manner, leading the way for reductions in other areas, such as plants and labor force.

Shrewd deletions can win on two fronts. Not only do they eliminate unprofitable products; they jettison unprofitable customers as well. Revlon, Inc., which recently implemented this strategy, has suffered losses for several years, even though it dominates cosmetics sales at mass-market stores, such as Target, Kmart, and Wal-Mart. Dealing with nearly $500 million in bank debt and $1.2 billion in bonds, the company seemingly adopted a strategy of shrinking sales.

Generally speaking, by lowering sales, a business reduces its funding needs, receives cash by liquidating its inventories and receivables, and gets rid of unprofitable products. For example, Revlon currently sells some 78 colors of nail polish, but it is dropping the number to 48. The risk, of course, is that it will lose more customers who want the discontinued colors than it will gain financially from reducing production, inventories, and distribution.

Revlon is shrinking by reducing expenditures on advertising and lowering the merchant's return allowance, but both methods can be risky if not watched carefully. It is hard to predict how much sales will fall when advertising budgets are slashed, or how merchants will react to no longer being able to return unsold items. Revlon may know the risk of losing its customers, but the true test is whether it eventually nets more profit—that is, the plan will have worked if what the corporation saves on advertising costs is more than what it loses in sales.

That product deletions are risky is worth repeating. Timing is always a factor, and trying to modify an unsuccessful deletion may be a wasted effort if your company isn't ready or willing to address the underlying strategic issues. Of course, during a crisis, it is likely that limited time and money will permit only the most superficial changes. Still, if they are innovative and skillfully enacted, product deletions can make a tremendous contribution to an organization's long-term health and help the product line achieve strategic goals, both immediately and in the future.

Product Characteristics

Products have three interconnected essential characteristics.

1. *Appearance* (including functionality) addresses the countless, often unpredictable, physical and emotional reactions of consumers to different products. Product taste, feel, and look are elements of appearance.

2. *Brand status* describes the degree to which a product's brand elevates it above identical or very similar competing goods. When they transcend commodity status and come to define a category, products become

very powerful brands. Kleenex brand tissues, Q-Tip brand ear swabs, and Xerox brand copies have all become product categories in themselves. Xerox is a common verb in English and other languages as well.

3. *Price responsiveness* is the degree to which raising or lowering an item's price affects its appeal. Called elasticity by economists, this trait measures how a price change alters consumers' buying decisions.

Let's look at these characteristics in more detail, one at a time.

Appearance

Of the three characteristics, appearance is probably the most important. But because it deals with customers' subjective perceptions, it is also the hardest to define and exploit. Like beauty, appearance resides in the eye of the beholder. A touch-up to its presentation can invigorate a tired product. The alteration doesn't have to make it look new; it can help it resemble a more successful item that already exists. It is no coincidence that the chips in most, if not all, brands of potato chips are approximately the same size, or that most new cars look alike. Also, marketing a product that controverts the current fashion or trend may generate business.

Another ploy is to change how the product is being offered: Sell 16-ounce bottles of soft drink when others offer 12; begin television shows five minutes after the hour and half-hour; or sell computers in a range of colors (as Apple Computer, Inc., markets the iMac). A final tactic to cure an ailing product is to offer a unique slant on it. Successful examples include the original and new Volkswagen Beetles and wraparound sunglasses.

By definition, certain items are identical regardless of who makes them. Few, if any, simple chemical compounds have yielded so much relief—or appeared in so many guises—as acetylsalicylic acid, otherwise known as aspirin. Since the palliative was discovered more than two thousand years ago in the bark of the willow tree, it has been chemically synthesized, mass produced, and widely prescribed. Neither its omnipresence nor everyone's familiarity with it have hindered companies from altering the compound's packaging or appearance so that it could be marketed as "new and improved."

Among its "innovations," aspirin has been buffered, enteric coated, reduced to children's size, and sold in a "heart-helpful" size. It is delivered as a gel cap, a time-release capsule, a liquid, chewing gum, or a plain white tablet. Packaging choices include single dosages, 10-packs, hundreds, and thousands.

Aspirin manufacturers make various claims of product differentiation in the hope of creating a brand out of a commodity, including the aspirin's purity, freshness, and the speed with which it will be absorbed into the bloodstream. For companies that sell aspirin, packaging matters as much as the product: It is the only way to make theirs stand out from the crowd.

Appearance affects the appeal of some products, but not all. The other two characteristics, brand status and price responsiveness, must always be taken into account. Appearance isn't a priority to consumers buying commodities. For example, shoppers don't care how table salt is packaged, as long as it meets certain basic expectations of price and unadulterated content. Thus, a commodity producer gains nothing by investing in appearance. Similarly, consumers purchasing a price-sensitive product, such as white computer paper, may bypass a high-priced sample that tries to attract attention with a handsome wrapper.

Brand Status

People pay more for desirable brands. Hence, becoming desirable is the pinnacle of a product's evolution. The possibility of elevating so-so, mediocre ones to strong brands should be examined during corporate transformation. Strong brands command higher prices even though the competition offers identical, lower-priced products.

Consider what Howard Schultz has done with coffee. Before he popularized the Starbucks brand, virtually every cup sold in the United States, except certain foreign kinds, cost about the same. Coffee was not always a profit center. Now, Starbucks Corporation sells a reportedly better cup of coffee for about triple what ordinary restaurants charge (or used to charge), and the brand is available on airplanes, in grocery stores, and at restaurants. In fact, these organizations carry Starbucks simply to benefit from its cachet and achieve its higher price point.

In addition to Starbucks, Perdue brand chicken, Poland Springs brand bottled water, Clorox brand bleach, Intel brand chips, and Crayola brand crayons have successfully escaped commodity status. Pets.com failed even after launching a multimillion-dollar advertising campaign featuring a sock puppet. The key to making the transition is marketing, marketing, and more marketing. It isn't necessary to produce the highest-quality product to establish a brand. Nor are the benefits of becoming a brand limited to national and regional products; the neighborhood pizza restaurant, for example, wants you to say, "Let's go to Marie's," instead of "Let's go out for pizza." Every establishment striving to be selected over its competitors is trying to become a brand.

Price Responsiveness

Zero price responsiveness is every company's dream: It means that prices can be raised at will, and consumers will continue to buy. For example, certain prescription medicines are priced at $5 to $50 per dose, even though they cost only a fraction of that to actually make. At the other extreme, an infinite price response, typical of commodities, means that the smallest alteration in price can provoke the consumer to change suppliers.

Advertising expenditures or gimmicks can tie consumers to a particular product and reduce price responsiveness. For example, some supermarket chains issue customers a card that attaches to their key rings. Scanned at checkout, the card gives them special discounts. Shoppers are so pleased by this system, which eliminates the tedium of clipping coupons, that few note the gimmick— that they are spending more than they might at a competing supermarket. Products with brand status are less price responsive than similar goods lacking a desirable brand, which explains why consumers are willing to pay more for certain brands of beer than for comparable beer from competing breweries. Likewise, a more attractive item is less vulnerable to price responsiveness.

Toyota Motor Corporation offers price discounts on Camrys that increase as the model ages. Yet few companies are aware of how sensitive their products are to price changes; either they change prices so seldom that elasticity can't be determined, or they don't pay adequate attention to the effects when they do alter prices.

In a seminal study, Charles Hofer observed that companies with highly differentiated products are able to raise prices without losing sales (C.W. Hofer, "Conceptual Constructs for Formulating Corporate and Business Strategies," no. 9-378-754, Intercollegiate Case Clearing House, Boston, 1977). He points out that, on a continuum, the differentiation of computer operating systems is very high, while that of sulfur or coal is on the low end. Breakfast cereals fall somewhere in the middle. Hofer argues that the more differentiated an enterprise's products are, the more liberty it has to raise prices.

Hofer categorizes consumers' motives for buying as economic (related to price), functional (related to what the product does), and psychological (what buyers hope it will do for them). Managers should know which of these three factors influences their customers.

According to Hofer, gasoline and groceries are economic purchases; computers, automobiles, and ballpoint pens are functional; and perfumes, fancy beauty salons, and designer clothing fall under the category of psychological products. Hofer emphasizes the rigidity of this system and believes that businesses have little, if any, ability to shift goods from one category to another.

Hofer's criteria can help companies manage the price responsiveness of their merchandise. Economic products are price responsive, while the psychological items are not. Enterprises that sell highly differentiated products that are purchased for psychological reasons, such as visits to a day spa or high-end bicycles, have the most flexibility in raising prices, while those that sell undifferentiated products that are bought for economic reasons, such as household bleach, have the least.

Hofer's paradigm helps us focus on the interconnectedness of the three product characteristics: appearance, brand status, and price responsiveness. If it is made more attractive and establishes itself as a brand, a product has, by definition, become more differentiated and therefore less price responsive. It may also acquire the characteristics of a psychological purchase, decreasing its price vulnerability.

Pricing Tactics

Raising prices is usually a necessary part of a Phoenix Effect effort; in a crisis, it is often the first step. Commodity products tend to be inflexible, but there may be a way to boost prices without arousing resistance. The aim is always to correct flaws in the pricing system and set prices at levels that benefit the organizations the most.

Historically, pricing decisions were made ad hoc, usually by the boss who decided when it was time to raise or lower prices. Today, pricing is its own field, replete with theories and experiments, some of which have revolutionized businesses and created profits where there were none.

One of the first proponents of creative pricing, the Gillette Company, sold razors below cost while making its profit by selling the blades separately. Until its instant camera became outdated, Polaroid Corporation did the same thing by selling the camera inexpensively, then making its profit on the film.

An aerospace designer and manufacturer takes near-zero profit margins on its jet engines and recovers revenues later on service and spare parts. The Korean company eMachines, Inc., takes this strategy even further. It nearly gives away its computer systems to people who contract to buy Internet access from it for three years. Within three months of launching this tactic, the organization's output jumped from zero to 200,000 units, catapulting it into the top tier of computer manufacturers.

Hewlett-Packard Company charges very little for printers, but profits handsomely from replacement ink cartridges. The idea is to reduce the consumer's up-front capital expense and to recover the revenue later by selling products or services that are necessary to operate the first purchase, and to do so after the customer has come to value and depend on the item.

The airline industry is an excellent example of how companies benefit from creative pricing strategies. From the inaugural flight of the Wright brothers in 1903 until 1991, the aggregate profitability of all U.S. airlines was negative; that is, taken together, they lost money. Then, in 1991, airlines adopted the pricing bucket paradigm, in which customers pay different prices for the same seat based on the traveler's needs. Businesspeople who need to reach their destinations quickly and without advance notice pay the highest prices, while leisure travelers with more flexibility and longer lead times get substantial discounts. More important, in the bucket model, some seats remain intentionally unsold, even when coach customers try to buy them, so that they will be available for last-minute, business-class travelers. Since implementing pricing buckets, airlines have increased their annual revenues by billions of dollars. Recently, car rental companies, hotels, and apartment buildings have adopted comparable pricing systems.

Another clever tactic is to price a product according to its perceived value. The more that people value it, the more they are willing to pay. Value pricing is especially useful to companies that offer several similar products that have the same cost structure. For example, stock traders using Ameritrade Holding Corporation's Ameritrade service pay $8 for a market order and $13 for a limit order. To Ameritrade, the cost differential between the two orders is negligible. But because limit orders set a precise trading price for transactions, while market orders take the offered price, investors place a higher value on the former. Hence, traders can charge more for them.

Businesses interview, role-play, and conduct experiments to establish what value customers place on particular items, but the outcomes remain imprecise. Astonishingly, AMR Corporation's American Airlines reportedly changes its prices as many as thousands of times a day, because among other reasons, the value of seats rises and falls in response to any number of internal and external factors.

Closely related to value pricing is limit pricing, wherein prices are set at or near the item's cost, stopping potential competitors from entering the market. A good example is the Weber-Stephen Products Co.'s Weber barbecue grill, which has cost nearly the same for years. That no comparable unit (with a similar kettle-heating technique) is on the market indicates that the grill's price is low enough to discourage competition. Though a higher price would yield higher profits in the short run, it might well diminish future profits if alternate brands stole some of Weber's customers.

Contrast Weber's limit pricing with the value pricing policy of Apple Computer. After pioneering the personal computer, Apple continued to charge about $5,000 per unit regardless of the falling costs of components. Today, Apple's market share is less than 3 percent, placing it behind nearly a dozen competitors. What happened? Other vendors, impressed with Apple's substantial profits on its early machines, developed competing products. The question some will ask is, had Apple applied limit pricing, would its aggregate profits have been greater and its market share stronger? Most significantly, it almost certainly would have attracted fewer competitors.

"Bundled pricing" is a tactic used to augment the sales of a slow-moving item by linking it to a faster moving, popular product. For example, a movie studio may force a theater to accept a film with uncertain prospects by bundling it with a blockbuster. In that way, the studio gains exposure for riskier projects.

Likewise, a clothing manufacturer may force retailers to buy shirts in a variety of colors when all they want are white and blue. Another bundling variation is to offer, say, three paintbrushes in a well-priced package when the consumer needs only one. If the bundle is priced correctly, the customer feels that he or she is getting a bargain and the company increases its sales. Still another version of this strategy is to offer a substantial discount on a popular item if the customer purchases one that has been recently introduced. In all these cases, the pricing algorithm gives shoppers an incentive to buy more than they had originally planned.

The loss leader, a time-tested pricing tactic, means that a product is sold below cost to stimulate profitable sales elsewhere in the enterprise. Thus, Burger King Corporation offers 99-cent chicken sandwiches; Southwest Airlines, Inc., sells $19 air fares; and the Ford Motor Company prices its least expensive car at or below cost. Loss leaders attract customers, demonstrate product quality, and create lifelong patrons. For Burger King, an ancillary objective is to earn an immediate profit when the consumer buys another item, such as a soda, at its ordinary price. Southwest and Ford earn their profits later when consumers return for a second purchase.

The final tactic of pricing strategy is setting the actual dollar figure, or "price point," at which it is best to sell your product. To determine them, smart companies closely scan the relevant landscape; then they conduct pricing surveys aimed at a particular market, in addition to "attitude" surveys to assess how customers feel about the appearance, brand, and price of their products as well as those of their competitors. A product's price, however, isn't entirely a marketing decision. It must cover costs and yield a profit. For example, an industry may include dozens of competitors that offer similar goods in the $250 to $350 price range. If your business decides to offer a product that caters to low-end consumers, say at $265, you must force its cost to align with that price, which we call target costs. Thus, establishing a price point enables the organization to manage its internal operations; it also provides leverage for negotiating input prices with suppliers.

Pricing tactics have virtually infinite permutations and can be adapted to any situation. If one tactic doesn't work, there is always another to try. As companies renew themselves, they must feel their way toward the pricing strategy that suits them best at any given time.

We suggest a general rule of thumb: When in trouble, raise prices.

Here's the corollary: If you expect bitter resistance or resentment to your move, find a pricing tactic that accomplishes what you need without the consumer noticing.

Having said that, we should also say that exceptions are inevitable. For retailer Fred, for instance, there are times when slashing prices—at least briefly on certain items— makes a lot of sense. Let's say Fred has an opportunity to balance its inventory by moving out a large amount of stock and, at the same time, give its best customers a break. However, if you do rid your warehouse of extra inventory, be very careful not to tamper with your existing sales volume. That is where people go wrong with this strategy. For example, you are overstocked with widgets and are about to call your Wal-Mart contact to tell her that next month all the widgets she can buy are 10 percent off. Don't do it, and here's why.

Once you tell someone that next month your prices will be lowered by 10 percent, you have indicated that the reduced pricing level applies to her regular 30,000 units. She isn't obligated to increase the volume of her purchase. You have blundered into having to reset both volume and price.

If you give a customer an extra 30,000 units for 50 percent off this month without stipulating that it is in addition to her current monthly purchase, don't be surprised when she cancels her regular order for the following month. All she has to do is pay a small cost for added warehouse space and she has received a half month's supply of widgets for free.

Instead, we suggest you say: "I see that you buy 30,000 units every month. If you'll buy an additional 30,000 units, I'll take 30 percent off the price, selling at 10 or 15 percent below our cost, as long as you maintain your regular order for the next three months." Your goal is always to move out stock over and above what the normal pace of your orders requires.

Raising prices can feel like a battle of wills. Keep in mind that your customers are loyal because they like dealing with you, which gives you an edge. They don't want to relinquish their relationships with you unless they are forced to do so—but, certainly, don't expect them to tell you that, and surely, don't put them in a position to have to leave you.

If it is an ordinary price increase intended to improve your margin, laying the groundwork in advance is the proper first step. If you are struggling to keep up with an unprecedented demand, tell your customers that your options are limited and none is cheap. Either you have to pay for overtime help or keep the plant open for a third shift—something you have never done before but that may be inevitable. Then, a month or two (two is preferred) before you intend to implement the increase, set the stage by having your salespeople spread the word that the company's recent growth is becoming nearly impossible to manage without effecting some sort of big change. This way, when you raise the price, your customers aren't caught off guard. They can present the increase in a company meeting by saying, "As you know, I have seen this coming for a while."

Common sense tells you that no one likes driving into a gas station at the moment the price signs are being increased. Clearly, people feel angry at the situation's arbitrariness; that is, had they arrived five minutes sooner, they would have received the fuel at the old price. That new gas prices are posted before 6:00 in the morning is deliberate and a facet of the psychology of pricing.

There is no point in denying that just about any time you raise prices, customers will ask why. If you care about their reactions, the worst possible response is, "I don't know. Management just told me." Of course, you may feel no need to justify the increase, but if you want customers to understand and accept a conspicuous price increase, you need a credible clarification, and that deserves some thought. Obviously, "We're not making the same amount of money that we used to" won't work. You want a plausible explanation that links your action to other well-known factors or situations that are causing costs to spiral upward. For example: "We have explored every reasonable alternative to raising our rates, but in the face of the soaring natural gas prices that are affecting us all, we have no choice." Another example: "Recruiting the best employees in this labor market has become extremely expensive given the salaries that the top 10 percent of university graduates can command."

To be sure, blaming someone or something else isn't always possible. It will most likely backfire if you are a public company issuing eagerly awaited earnings reports. It is one thing when gasoline costs more because the Organization of Petroleum Exporting Countries (OPEC) is bumping up the price of oil, a situation that receives a lot of press coverage, but it is understandably quite another when one of the big U.S. oil companies reports a 30 or 40 percent rise in profits. Among other problems, consumers will begin to talk about boycotting that organization.

While the average angry consumer may be more talk than action, boycotts of 100,000 people have occurred. Likewise, if you are that oil company's largest customer, you may end up resenting the fact that its earnings are up so much.

In such a case, our advice to most businesses is straightforward: Call your biggest customers and tell them you're dropping your prices. It doesn't have to be a 30 or 40 percent decrease; 3 percent will work. The point is to adjust your prices before they realize you are increasing margins. This is the most compelling argument against letting your finance people issue earnings information without first considering the public relations ramifications. While the analysts will praise the margin and profit jump, your customers may be irritated, especially if their own profits are up 5 percent and yours are up 50.

Of course, if your earnings are down X percent, which you can explain by increases in your labor or raw material costs, raising your own prices isn't likely to evoke negative public relations. Of course, customers won't like it, but, after all, neither do you when your role is that of the consumer.

Some enterprises will do almost anything to prevent their products from becoming commodities for which they can no longer charge premium prices. Diamonds are such products. Huge warehouses in Russia and South Africa that stockpile unsold diamonds attest to ways that a cartel keeps a market from becoming competitive and demonstrates the tremendous profits that monopolists earn when they do their work well.

If you take from this chapter only one point, it should be this: In a Phoenix Effect effort, products and strategy are inseparable, like interwoven threads of the same fabric. In the same way, product characteristics and pricing tactics are inextricably entwined, making it possible to consider each only as it relates to the other within this interconnected system.

CHAPTER 9

Produce the Product

You have come up with a surefire product and marketing plan. All you need now is a squad of accountants to start calculating your profits.

Not so fast. What will you need to bring your product into existence, and if it is successful, how can you ensure that it continues to be?

You are encountering one of the oldest problems in business: a manufacturing plant. Historically, plant has referred to physical assets—land, buildings, and equipment—but now it also has come to include intellectual property, such as the computer programs that guide automated manufacturing.

The relationship between your plant and your product has everything to do with the long-term success of your business. We begin the discussion by asking three interrelated questions.

1. *Does your plant serve the needs of your product?* If it does not, what must you change in order to facilitate the swifter, cheaper, or more uniform production of your merchandise? In our view, the answer is by constantly monitoring and adjusting the plant's "input mix," the term we use for the multitude of things (raw materials, equipment, supplier contracts) that are required to run your plant. Addressing this issue appropriately means that you never abandon the quest for better, faster, and cheaper alternatives for all of the inputs.

2. *Should you combine operations with some other company, even a competitor?* If growth seems too heavy a burden to take on right now, why not share the load? A partnership can definitely work to your advantage on goals such as maximizing capacity.

3. *Should you outsource?* We advise taking this question to extremes: Do you really need any plant at all? Can you move everything onto the Internet? Then, why outsource anything? Outsourcing, unfortunately, often leads to plants closings, which can be badly mishandled.

These plant-related issues, which we will discuss in detail, form the heart of this chapter. But we want to preface that discussion with some cautionary words about efficiency and automation. Here, as all new managers learn, appearances can be deceiving, and there are no easy answers.

Efficiency and Automation Have Their Limits

It is an accepted fact that new efficiencies and automation in manufacturing plants can yield handsome benefits. In some of these instances, however, the lucrative results may be short term. Azteca Production International, Inc.'s Sasson Jeans is an example. By assembling its jeans from front to back versus left to right, it was able to cut out a number of production steps. The old system had the left and right sides coming down the line on opposite ends of the plant. With studies, Sasson discovered that if one line made the back of the jeans and the other line made the front, and then the two pieces were sewn together on the outsides and insides of the legs, it could save precious manufacturing time per pair of jeans.

But Sasson Jeans wanted to find additional efficiencies. The rising cost of human labor compelled the U.S. jeans maker to move manufacturing to Puerto Rico, where labor costs were lower and tax advantages were available. But over the years, rising wages there caused Sasson to pick up stakes again and relocate most of its production operations to Mexico. Where do such company migrations stop? How many inexpensive labor pools have not yet been tapped?

Many businesspeople continue to believe that increasingly sophisticated automation will keep labor and other manufacturing expenses under control and widen profit margins as well. The worm in this apple is the time it takes to build an automated system for any given product. If you go to an industry trade show and explain your problem, the equipment manufacturers will tell you what they have, why it will solve your problem, and how little, relatively, it will cost you. But what the cost-benefit presentation doesn't cover are the special demands you will make on the machines.

Suppose, for example, your product requires that you change the color of thread 19 times during the day. If each thread change means that the machine will be down for half an hour, you have 9.5 hours of downtime every day. Your particular needs drastically reduce the economic advantage of automation and enhance the appeal of relocating to less expensive labor markets.

While equipment manufacturers can usually custom build machines that will solve major downtime problems, such as the thread changes, one-of-a-kind automated systems are expensive and may take years to bring online. That means you have to assume that years from now, your customers will be ordering the same or higher quantities of the same product. If they switch, you have made a big plant investment for a diminished market.

Sun Coast Closures, Inc., is an example of a company that has been able to remove labor intensity by investing in custom automation equipment when, and only when, it has commitments from big volume buyers. (Closures are caps or lids—a bottle top or a butter container lid.) Such buyers, which sell hundreds of millions of items requiring closures every year, look to the closure industry for quality control and consistency in color and fit.

Sun Coast keeps the quality of its manufacturing high and its costs low by automating just about everything it does. For the entire process, from the time the rail car drops off the plastic pellets to the moment the finished caps, tops, and lids are packed for shipping, rarely does any human being touch the closures.

It is a fascinating story of superior quality and automation, but even more interesting is that Sun Coast tries to watch its revenues, not allowing any one customer's business to exceed a small percentage of its annual revenue. Though this business practice may cost Sun Coast some business, the corporation prefers to be insulated from the difficulties, adversities, and problems that would result from losing a customer that accounted for, say, 40 percent of its revenue, including immediate layoffs and the idleness of expensive machinery.

Many companies don't exercise Sun Coast's self-discipline in refusing to be excessively dependant on one or a few large customers. And they can vanish overnight. For example, let's say a company, thrilled to pick up a huge Wal-Mart Stores, Inc., order, drops its smaller customers to accommodate it. Then, the very next year, Wal-Mart hires a new buyer who doesn't like the product. It could be a quick death: From around-the-clock shifts this week to out of business the next.

The good news is that sudden death can be prevented by long-term planning that focuses intently on plant issues. Such planning is critical because plant expenditures account for the majority of corporate investment dollars. Unfortunately, a company in crisis seldom has time to deal with long-term problems; addressing them must wait until quick fixes have been applied and a genuine turnaround or transformation is under way.

We have already touched, by example, on many of the kinds of decisions involving a plant that must be faced by a corporation bent on turnaround. They include the number, size, and location of facilities; the timing, financing, and valuation of equipment upgrades and replacements;

environmental and related land-management concerns; and, often these days, the formulation and implementation of "virtual" business concepts. All these decisions, in keeping with the long life of most plant assets, should consider risk and return from a long-term perspective, looking past cyclical prices and market perturbations. Avoid the temptation of going for a high return that exposes you to excessive risk. It is a poor business decision that could threaten your entire company.

Now let's look at the first of the three major issues you must face if you really want to make your company's physical assets work for, not against, you. It is all about what it takes to manage the collection of things and ever-changing circumstances that make up your corporate plant.

Managing the Inputs That Shape Your Plant

Brick-and-mortar facilities and reliable equipment are just two of several resources required for the production of goods or the delivery of services. Others include labor (managerial, technical, and functional); materials, both raw (e.g., crude oil or flour) and finished (e.g., semiconductors or outsourced goods); and utilities and other standard or recurring expenses, such as telecommunications, energy, and transportation. Each product carries its own potential manufacturing efficiencies and inefficiencies. Moreover, no facility exists in a theoretical vacuum, and such factors as land values, environmental sensitivity, and cultural values of the local people (e.g., small town versus large city) must be explored.

Management tries to combine all these inputs so that the cost of the output is as low as possible. The goal is always to reduce costs by substituting a less expensive input. The degree to which that can be done varies across industries.

At first glance, land would appear to be something for which there is no substitute. But managers at Pathmark Stores, Inc., have been clever in making the most of land values. Supermarkets are simple physical structures with relatively low construction costs. The major expenses of operating them are inventory and land. With suburban land values reaching peak levels, supermarket construction is moving toward sites with surprisingly low costs: inner cities. Pathmark opened a 32,000-square-foot store in the Bedford-Stuyvesant area of Brooklyn, New York, in 1997 at a cost of slightly more than $1 million. With sales of $30 million per year, the unit is the second-best performer in the entire Pathmark chain. Had Pathmark not moved quickly to capitalize on cost-saving land values, the residents of this area might not have a convenient supermarket.

Intense competition accelerates the need to fix up, remodel, and replace equipment and buildings. Everyone is familiar with Burger King Corporation, a unit of Diageo PLC, with nearly 11,000 restaurants worldwide, 75 percent of which are in the United States. Although customers visit Burger King for fast food, the plant (that is, the building, parking lot, drive-through area, and interior furnishings) has to tempt them to come in. In Burger King's highly competitive market, an old-fashioned physical plant (some Burger King restaurants are 40 years old) impedes product marketing. One reason for the disparity between annual sales at the typical Burger King ($1.1 million) and a comparable McDonald's ($1.6 million) may be Burger King's retention of some older stores. Planning for the twenty-first century, it created a prototypical restaurant that deviates totally from the old look. Elongated, not square, the building's exterior has a bright, almost carnival-like color scheme; it has an interactive playground and a drive-through area with its own kitchen to reduce customers' waiting time. The new design is more expensive, but if it elevates Burger King's sales, the funds are well spent.

During a crisis, reinvesting in plants is usually suspended to conserve cash, a step that rarely causes much damage in the short run. Eventually, however, skimping on plant upkeep extracts a toll that becomes apparent in equipment breakdowns and crumbling infrastructure.

In their search for less expensive alternatives for the wide array of plant inputs, managers typically focus first on how machines can reduce labor and material costs. Though this is perfectly valid, they should remember that machines aren't a panacea, as we saw in the example of Sasson Jeans.

The search for cost-saving substitutes spreads beyond the factory floor and eventually includes every producer of goods or services. For example, airlines have increased their orders for jumbo aircraft that can hold more passenger seats and are installed with more automated flight systems (which require smaller crews), which means that their employees are more productive. Similarly, the shift to personal computers in offices and factories translates into reduced labor expenditures. Additional businesses begin to adopt one or another alternative as soon as the positive effects of doing so become apparent.

Cost should always be the major factor underlying input substitutions, which explains why human labor is sometimes preferred over machines. Traditionally, factories in the southern United States have had fewer machines and employed more workers than their counterparts in the North. More recently, lower labor costs (sometimes less than one-fiftieth of U.S. rates) account for decisions to establish factories in East Asia and Mexico. The same is true for computer programming and telecommunications services that relocate offshore in places such as India and Ireland. Driving the quest for substitutions is a desire to find cost reductions before the competition does.

Opportunities for substituting inputs with less expensive alternatives are practically inexhaustible and constrained only by managers' willingness to pursue them. Don't forget to look in the most mundane places: Reduce the amount of wasted material; use a machine that requires less service and has fewer parts to replace; find a cheaper material that will do the job. Similarly, you may be unintentionally paying costs or purchasing utilities and services that exceed the going competitive rates. More diligent monitoring followed by quick intervention can virtually eliminate such needless losses.

Running a factory requires that you balance how close to its maximum productive output your plant operates. Too far below 100 percent capacity results in a high cost structure, because capital charges are distributed across a relatively low output level. Peak production, that is, too high a utilization level, overheats the system. Costs rise as new inputs are hastily added to stimulate output and avoid shortages, which will disappoint and anger consumers. Inevitably, quality suffers and more investment dollars are thrown at the problem.

Yet such crises can be avoided. An intelligent rearrangement of equipment or procedures can create new capacity. For example, moving airplane seats closer together allows an airline to board more passengers. Of course, any change that adversely affects your customers' convenience or comfort, risks alienating them and is best done when competitors are also doing it.

A seemingly simple change in procedures can also enlarge capacity significantly. When a taxi company decided to change the oil in its cabs every 6,000 miles instead of every 3,000, the extended time between maintenance appointments had the effect of raising the number of cabs it had on the street at any given time.

Toyota Motor Corporation has come up with a way to simultaneously raise capacity in one area while lowering it in another, and at the same time eliminating plants. The Japanese carmaker's plan is brilliant. It is modifying all of its factories, worldwide, so that it can rapidly switch over from manufacturing cars and trucks for its many domestic markets to producing them for export. When car sales fall in Brazil, for example, and rise in the United States, Toyota will use its plant in Brazil to produce cars for the United States. In other words, Toyota will put its Brazilian plant to work as a U.S. plant; in so doing, it simultaneously manages to lose nothing on Brazil's drop in sales and capitalize on the growth in U.S. sales.

Combining Operations: The Sharing Option

A more radical method for creating greater capacity combines several operations—run by different, otherwise independent companies—in the same physical space. This eliminates the need for individual businesses to install a full accoutrement of facilities. An example is a food court in a mall in which as many as 10 individual stands share seating and maintenance costs.

In many of GC Companies, Inc.'s General Cinema theaters, customers can eat their dinners as they watch a first-run movie. What used to be an ordinary candy counter now has a pint-size Pizza Hut and a Taco Bell restaurant beside it. These specialty-menu operations share the real estate with popcorn machines and candy racks without taking up additional plant space or increasing the theater's costs. Yet they rack up sizable sales. In combining operations that target the consumer sector, the key is to blend complementary products; that is, few moviegoers would bring dry cleaning or undeveloped film to a theater, but the same people might buy a movie poster or a taco.

Similarly, individual physicians share expenses for special medical equipment, disabled person access, Internet wiring, and lab services in addition to office quarters. Internet service providers (ISPs) are also sharing. An ISP must have a point of presence (POP) in each local market it serves so that clients can access the Internet with a local phone call. But building so many special facilities would be prohibitively expensive. The solution is to rent space for a computer tower that processes phone calls. One ISP, Concentric Network Corporation, rents closet space from Payless ShoeSource, Inc., which has thousands of shoe store locations across the country. Payless receives rental fees and Concentric minimizes its investment in physical plants.

Combining or sharing factories, space, and other physical assets is beneficial during all stages of the Phoenix Effect—crises, turnarounds, and transformations. Subleasing extra space to a tenant, filling a neighbor's partially empty delivery truck, or sharing a mainframe computer are all examples of opportunities that present themselves to creative managers.

Many managers are hesitant to discuss the issue of combining operations with their competitors. Experience has taught us that if you want to have such a conversation, it is best to do so directly to avoid arousing suspicion about your motives. You can call a competitor and say something like, "Look, we both know that the economy has hit our industry hard. We both have production plants that we are considering closing. Why should we close both plants? I could lease you or you could lease me X percentage of production capacity and the workforce required." It sounds almost too easy to actually work, but it is worth a try.

Still, if you feel too awkward or that the situation is particularly sticky, hire a third party to be your intermediary. Someone who has an investment banking or comparable background is a good choice and will take a similar approach: "We're looking for solutions, and we see that your earnings, like ours, have been down; we would like to know if you have any interest in trying to work something out?" Probably the first thing your competitor will say is, "What do you have in mind?"

An advantage to hiring intermediaries is that they protect you if your competitor thinks combining forces is a terrible idea. You can disavow any knowledge of their proposal.

Combining purchasing operations is something that is being considered by Hilton Group, plc, Marriott International, Inc., and others. These corporations are coordinating their buying power into one large operation. By using one group of purchasing managers, they will gain a substantial negotiating advantage they didn't previously have. From the perspective of consolidating costs, this venture is cutting edge and a strong argument for opening up discussions with a competitor.

When—and When Not—to Outsource

Our experience is that, for certain problems, outsourcing is often the perfect solution. Still, it isn't without its pitfalls, which we discuss at the end of this section.

Increasing the margins on the products you have chosen to move forward is the best reason to outsource. If after receiving bids on your manufacturing job, you are convinced that outsourcing of some kind will lower your plant costs without compromising the product's quality, you face some difficult decisions. The first two may be which of your plants it makes the most sense to close and whether you should get out of manufacturing altogether? As you assess these issues, we suggest you bear in mind that doing your own manufacturing gives you the advantage of quick reaction time. When you outsource, especially to offshore operations, you lose control over the timing, but you can gain tremendous cost advantages if—and only if—your customers are willing to wait a little longer for their orders. The questions are complex, and, as we keep saying, there are no easy answers.

If you own a plant that is too big for your business, you have a white elephant on your hands. Sometimes it is just as difficult and costly to find an appropriately sized plant as it is to abandon production altogether. If you are going to sell a plant, we suggest you make no renovations first. Fixtures and other associated improvements usually hold little, if any, value to a new owner or lessee and can muddy negotiations.

The question of whether it is necessary to own or lease a plant at all underlies most decisions about the appropriateness of outsourcing. Remember, companies that have no plants continue to market products; they just don't manufacture them. They simply transfer that task to other organizations. Needless to say, most employees will react negatively to the idea of outsourcing since their jobs are at stake.

During labor negotiations with its pilots in late 1998, FedEx Corporation announced its intention of using foreign airlines to carry international delivery packages. If the plan had been enacted, international services would have been outsourced to charter airlines using non-FedEx crews. Eventually, under an agreement with the union, the plan was shelved. But it may someday reemerge as FedEx seeks new ways to increase its profitability and, at the same time, do away with some of its physical assets.

Sensitive labor-management issues such as those at FedEx make it important to clarify the process that has led you to consider outsourcing. Be sure that you aren't mistaking a plant problem for something else. For example, a restaurant that has people waiting for hours may have too little space, and too few tables, or a bottleneck in the kitchen. The first two are plant issues and though the third may be, it could also be a process issue. However, a slow maître d' is a people issue. And food that is priced too low is a product issue.

Outsourcing is one way to avoid dealing with assets that no longer quite fit your business. It may also provide an opportunity to enter new businesses in which your expertise is limited. For example, a personal computer manufacturer may outsource in-home service to a company specializing in that. If the arrangement proves mutually profitable, the PC maker may sell its in-home service business, along with related facilities and equipment, to the organization it had been outsourcing to. The PC company reduces its investments in fixed assets and inventory and improves its working capital, while the outsourced enterprise gains a business that has already demonstrated its profitability.

Outsourcing is a way to increase capacity. For example, Dr. Ing. hc F. Porsche AG sells a car under its own name that it doesn't make. Though made by a competitor, it is branded for Porsche. It is part of an experiment Porsche is conducting to determine if it should stay in the manufacturing business or move into the label and image business. A lot of organizations are struggling with the same issue. The key is to figure out where your expertise—that is, your core competency—lies. If your history is marketing, finance, or sales, then the last thing you want to take on is running a plant and vice versa.

Moving a business onto the Internet, whether or not it is in conjunction with an outsourcing effort, is another way to finesse certain plant costs. One worker, a computer server, and a monitor can replace many of the functions of a large plant that houses employees and inventory. The tasks of making the product, filling the orders, shipping to customers, handling returns, and servicing repairs are handled in-house or outsourced, depending on costs and the corporation's history and mission. While the main risk of outsourcing is that your supplier will become your competitor, the primary risk of Web commerce is that you compete in a sphere with few barriers to entry. However, even with a physical plant, lacking an Internet presence makes you vulnerable to a Web-savvy competitor who can steal your clientele.

In a totally virtual business, everything involved in providing the service and manufacturing and handling the products is outsourced, and all interactions between the company and its customers are electronic. The Internet has enabled some companies to change their business models. For example, a bike manufacturer can stop making bicycles and just sell them without having to warehouse, handle, or in fact, even see them.

Wal-Mart is now present on the Internet. This behemoth's $190 billion in annual sales represents the spoils of victories in the mass merchandise, warehouse store, and grocery store markets. In each case, Wal-Mart employed the same strategy: superior logistics and lower prices. Now, unsurprisingly, Wal-Mart executives are attracted to the new frontier of the Web. As we have said, serving customers on the Internet requires less physical plant space, and Wal-Mart is extending that strategy still further by outsourcing its way onto the Web. It hired Books-A-Million, Inc., to provide books for its online bookstore, and Fingerhut Companies, Inc., a division of Federated Department Stores, Inc., to process and handle all of its Internet orders. In addition to diminishing the need for physical space, this plan benefits Wal-Mart by relieving it of the tedious responsibility of coordinating Internet logistics.

Wal-Mart is relying on outsiders with expertise to teach it about this new market. Books-A-Million operates a successful Internet bookstore; Fingerhut, the country's second largest seller of catalog items, is expert at home delivery— the most difficult aspect of online retailing. Wal-Mart may decide later not to work with partners, but for now it is coming online with almost no assistance from its plants.

Learning to manage outsourced work, however, requires a long learning curve; hence, if you are going to relinquish your plants, do so gradually. Though you may be outsourcing the production of your goods, you are still responsible for their quality if they come out under your name. Moreover, the management task is made more, not less, difficult by the fact that production is becoming increasingly concentrated in the hands of fewer, larger, and more specialized organizations with high-volume outputs and economies of scale.

An interesting phenomenon can occur if a huge manufacturer decides it no longer wants to produce other companies' brands. Managers start thinking that if their enterprise was producing its own line, instead of, say, Levi Strauss & Co.'s Levi brand jeans, it would be holding on to a considerable margin. But do they realize the problems of warehousing? What about when people place orders for volumes of merchandise that they then don't take? When myriad crises hit, they frequently decide that being the label maker isn't what they had hoped. Though vertical integration—which is what we are talking about—served John D. Rockefeller very well a hundred years ago, controlling products from raw material to sale isn't how most businesses work today. When profits shrink and continue to shrink, it may be because the business has fundamental problems for which vertical integration is not the solution. There is a saying we like very much that applies here: Artificial intelligence is no match for natural stupidity. Stick with what you know.

Something else you should know: Most manufacturers have an imprint or sign that identifies their products. Some place a tiny telltale wiggle or line in a pattern. Some of the symbols are known by consumers; others aren't. In the plastic drinkware industry, every plant does something a little bit differently, so that it is always possible to discern one manufacturer's product from another's as they sit side by side on the shelf. It may be a mark etched into the mold, which you won't see if you don't know exactly where to look, but it is there.

Our point is this: If you are working with an overseas manufacturer because it dramatically lowers your cost margins, be prepared for the fact that, before long, that company's identity will be known throughout your industry. There are few big secrets in business and even fewer in international trade. It is possible that you will lose your advantage and perhaps some customers when they discover the source of your deals.

Again, we think that sticking to what you do best is vital. Each party in the value chain adds something to the process, and you lose that if you cut that party out. Can one enterprise be a successful manufacturer, wholesaler, retailer, and a label, as well? Some can, but they are few. The watchword on outsourcing is caution. Beware of easy answers.

Closing Plants

No discussion of physical assets would be complete without a comment about closing plants. Whether they are the result of combining operations, outsourcing, moving onto the Internet, or the end of a business, plant shutdowns are inevitable.

When the choice is whether or not to close the plant, we always tell managers to select the option that they have not tried before. We want to push them out of their comfort zones. Like almost everyone else, managers instinctively do what has worked in the past. But of course every new situation requires and deserves a thorough analysis and is likely to evoke new, previously unasked questions. Is it necessary to lay off people? Should we call our competitors before we make this decision? Why are we assuming we need to sell this plant?

Although closing a facility can be practically insignificant if plenty of job opportunities are available, you must be prepared for the worst, by which we mean incidents of violence. People will be angry and you need to ensure that you don't leave yourself open to being its target. We advise that on the day you announce the closing, you rent a car, because, if employees are familiar with yours, it is possible you will find your tires slashed, or worse. Don't underestimate the need for security. Carter experienced a very frightening plant closing:

> After we announced that we had to shut down, one employee went out to his car, where he had a shotgun, and came back with it looking for me. I had already left

for lunch and received a call from security on my cell phone. I was told he was waiting for me. I told the security officer to tell him to stay right there, and I would be back in 15 minutes. And I was but had the police in front of me as I entered the building.

There are U.S. laws designed precisely to protect workers in the event of factory closings, and you should follow those statutes exactly, without the slightest variation. Also, consult with labor lawyers before, not after, you announce the closing.

When a plant closes but the business remains intact at other locations, there will be invaluable people whom you will want to keep. They may include two or three assistant plant managers as well as a few highly skilled, specialized machinists. Therefore, before the factory actually shuts, prepare wage and benefit packages for them that could entice them to stay with the company by moving to a different site.

Closing a factory is always sad and usually difficult, both emotionally and logistically. Even if you are shutting down for a good reason—say, you are looking forward to becoming an entirely virtual organization—the closing marks an end to the hopes and excitement you felt when you first opened it or took it over. In fact, most people feel this decision to be a choice for the lesser of two evils, and probably no one closes a factory without mixed emotions. Undoubtedly, you will experience a loss, but you may risk too many other losses if you keep it running. Our experience has taught us that the best way to make this judgment is to ask probing questions, don't accept the obvious answers, and analyze every and all open options.

CHAPTER 10

Change the Process

It was a bad day at Sun Coast Closures, Inc. The trouble, as it turned out, had everything to do with process. One of the company's biggest customers had received a bid from a supplier offering to make container caps at a couple of cents per unit less than what Sun Coast was charging. Their message: Match that price or risk losing the account. Sun Coast was staring at the possible evaporation of a huge chunk of business: millions of caps a year.

The entire management team was astounded. Sun Coast was used to having to shave, say, tenths of a cent off its prices—but a couple of cents per little cap seemed outrageous. Carter thought to himself, "That supplier wants to steal the business and is willing to sell caps at or certainly below cost in order to get it. We ought to call their bluff and see if there really is a supplier at that price."

But you have to face reality and start to think practically, and Carter and the people at Sun Coast did. They took several steps immediately. First, they convinced Sun Coast engineers to take this challenge very seriously. Then, they tried to get a copy of the less expensive closure, which is the best way to answer the questions racing through everyone's minds: What is the logical explanation for the competitor's cut-rate cap? Is this a bluff? Has there been a breakthrough of some kind? Or is it the equivalent of a car without horns, wheels, and a steering wheel? Sun Coast Closures has the highest reputation for quality in the industry and was positive that the customer would not go for a reduced quality closure. But where to look for savings.

Before long, Sun Coast's engineers figured out that the price reduction could only come out of labor costs. All the other expenses, such as raw materials and machinery maintenance and repair, could not have been cut dramatically enough to explain this. Sun Coast had to find a process that reduced the labor required for producing closures; that was clearly the only option.

Sun Coast found what it was looking for in its long-standing practice of using sharp-eyed quality control people to spot defective caps as they came down the conveyor belt in a single line. Identifying and throwing away the faulty ones was an essential quality control process. But could it be automated without sacrificing quality?

The answer was yes. Engineers installed special equipment to replace the workers who inspected the closures. Images of each closure were fed to a computer and matched against a quality control perfect composite of an acceptable closure. A failed match indicated a defective cap, and the computer would trigger a device that pulled that closure off the line and into the trash can.

Thus, process innovation allowed the organization to achieve what had first seemed impossible, and saved the day for Sun Coast Closures.

We are frequently asked how we identify a process problem, as opposed to an issue of working capital, scope, orientation, or any other trouble area. The truth is that processes are usually ignored until an external event makes it impossible to avoid them. What happened at Sun Coast is typical. It is human nature to need a compelling reason, even a crisis, to change.

Also, when you are running an enterprise, urgent matters come up every day, to which process analysis and improvement always seem to take a back seat. Only the most affluent corporations can afford a permanent staff assigned specifically to research and develop process improvements.

However, process issues will instantly overshadow every other priority when a critical customer mandates you to come in at, say, 6 percent less "if you want to renew your contract for next year." Then you have a choice. You appeal either to your engineers, as Sun Coast did, or to your own suppliers, maybe starting with your shipping-carton maker, and say, "We pay $1.98 per unit for this shipping box; you have to figure out how to charge us $1.40, if you want to keep our business."

What you are doing is pushing the pressure backward to find a cheaper, lighter-weight box. And, in our experience, most of the time your supplier will agree without a huge argument, which, of course, makes you wonder why this solution wasn't offered before. But, in fact, you know why. Until now, he had no incentive to do so because you were happy with the product.

Of course, an immediate "yes" may not be the best response to a client who asks to pay less for your product. You might equivocate a bit, perhaps say you aren't sure that this can be done, but you will be glad to take a look. Never say, "No, we won't consider it." Always leave the door open a crack to negotiate.

Process Improvement ABCs

Many systems and numerous consultants are available to help you when you encounter a process problem. Many consulting firms advocate business process reengineering (BPR), a concept rooted in Michael Hammer's and James Champy's theory, argued in their book *Reengineering the Corporation,* that business should be organized by process, not by task. BPR's methodology addresses mainly (though not exclusively) larger corporations, urging them to invest aggressively in information technology as a way of reducing reliance on human effort. During many corporate transformations, BPR has proven its worth by catapulting companies over difficult obstacles.

For organizations involved in turnaround or crisis management, ordinary process improvements, or OPIs, are a less disruptive alternative that is often sufficient. Implementing OPIs, designed to correct process faults, requires at the outset little more than a probing eye and a determination to improve. As a rule, OPI modifications involve simple transitions from less efficient to more efficient methods.

Inefficiency is the fundamental process error, and the results include wasted time, lost money, and poor quality. We contend that all process errors are avoidable, and if they already exist, they can be corrected. (Deeply entrenched and long-standing errors may require substantial time and money to fix.) The fact that process errors are considered inevitable in some industries makes them less, not more, forgivable. If process flaws are tolerated, then no amount of vigilance and ingenuity can protect against them, and they become a formidable barrier to success. For example, if a baseball team has great players, clever coaches, and loyal fans, but is unable to win a pennant, it should examine its processes (such as late-season physical conditioning and farm-team player development) for hidden flaws. Similarly, an enterprise with higher costs or lower revenues than those of a direct competitor may be a victim of process errors, which really amount to failures of execution.

Such failures must be eliminated, and the first step is to identify the ordinary process problems, no matter how minor they may seem; the second is to correct them. OPIs that require little investment or sophistication, not surprisingly, deliver modest gains. But a number of small improvements, taken one step at a time, can yield a significant overall improvement in the company's performance, including increased production, saved time and money, and diminished waste. Costing little or nothing and requiring minimal employee retraining, OPI opportunities arise repeatedly as a company renews itself.

For instance, after a colleague of ours bought an ornamental spoon manufacturer, he spent an afternoon at the plant and observed the following sequence of events: An employee watched a stamping machine churn out spoons. After some amount of time, he turned off the machine and walked 75 feet to a supply room. There, he picked up boxes and cotton for packaging the spoons, carried them back to the machine, and restarted the machine to begin the cycle again. What was the new owner's OPI? Simply shelve empty boxes and cotton beside the worker. Immediately, machine downtime as well as wasted employee time declined by 25 percent. This inefficient process had been in place and, most likely, unquestioned for 30 years. Such opportunities for process improvements are more common than you might imagine, but keep one caveat in mind: Sometimes employees are aware of long-standing inefficiencies and know how to conceal them if they know the boss is watching. So, keep your presence as inconspicuous as possible.

OPIs can correct three troubled areas: wasted activity time, pointless costs, and inferior product quality. (The example in the spoon factory illustrates a wasted-time OPI.) You will see gains from OPIs, both quantitatively in lower costs and qualitatively in better customer relations.

In an organization that encourages open communication among all levels, valuable OPI suggestions can come from employees, customers, and suppliers. If attentively and fairly administered, a program of financial rewards or other kinds of individual recognition stimulates the flow of OPI ideas.

Examples of effective OPIs can be found in almost every successful business. We will look at some of our favorites later in this chapter, which is organized into time-related OPIs, cost-related OPIs, and quality-enhancing OPIs. To a large extent, these three areas of process improvement are interrelated. Wasting time raises costs, and finding cheaper ways of conducting business will, most likely, also save time and improve efficiency, all of which make quality control easier to manage.

Time-Efficient Processes

Though "time is money" is very true, time is also a hidden business cost because it isn't broken down separately on the income statement. Wasted time is buried in higher wages or in the costs of desperate overnight shipping to meet a deadline. Without separate reports for how time is consumed, it is impossible to measure how much of it is wasted.

The kinds of ordinary business activities that are particularly time-consuming include producing goods or services, designing new product platforms, modifying factory lines to enable new production, taking orders, attending meetings, writing reports, and moving and storing inventories and finished products. Observing the flow of regular activities like these will frequently reveal opportunities to cut out wasted time. Many managers get ideas for time-saving OPIs by walking the floor, listening to telephone conversations, observing group meetings, and talking to workers. Some employees invariably resist the idea of improving efficiency because they view it as a potential threat to their jobs; or they may feel that talking to a manager will brand them as a snitch or company stooge in the eyes of their fellow workers. Educating employees about the importance of efficient processes may reduce this kind of resistance.

Because standard accounting statements don't report time consumed as such, some enterprises create their own time-consumption databases. For example, to understand the average time it takes to bring new products to market, companies measure how long a certain number of workers spends on specialized repetitive tasks. They do this for a number of new products. The objective isn't to define rigid time frames by which to govern future efforts. That, in itself, would be a waste of time, because every project is different—some are more urgent than others, some merely exploratory, and each is assigned a different team. Instead, the objective is to create a metric that can be used to recognize departures from the norm. The underlying reasons for exceptional time consumption, whether perceived as too long or too short, become clear when the details are studied further. If open communication is part of the company culture, employees are more likely to make suggestions that can increase efficiency in the future.

That the value of the metric lies in its ability to reveal unusual expenditures of time deserves repeating. It should not be used as a goad by managers or as a challenge to project teams obsessed with completing a process in new record time. Speed achieved at the expense of quality is likely to end up costing more time. Misusing such metrics may be a valid reason for withholding them from the company as a whole. They might be more helpful if shared on a need-to-know basis. Of course, doing things faster should never be an excuse for sloppiness and errors.

The quest for time efficiency motivates, in part, JIT inventory control, a recent, powerful management innovation. An organization that uses JIT has practically no inventory and saves the time it used to spend ordering, cataloging, inspecting, storing, and delivering stock. With JIT, inventories arrive and are brought directly to the right person exactly when they are needed.

Westinghouse Air Brake Company increased production per worker by 10 times more per day during the eight years between 1991 and 1999. Its secret weapon was *kaizen*—the Japanese technique of continuous improvement. Westinghouse's choices as the 1990s began were stark: Either it had to improve efficiency or move its operations out of the country. *Kaizen* is a formalized version of the OPI method. At several scheduled times a year, management requests that the entire workforce devote itself to improving ordinary processes: Some modifications are radical; others are evolutionary and barely cause a ripple. At the heart of *kaizen* is the belief that savings lurk everywhere. One of Westinghouse's most beneficial changes was "single-piece flow," which adjusts the factory's output to the rate at which consumers buy the product. When production and sales are synchronized, there are no finished-goods inventories. This means that inventory costs are lower and write-offs attributable to obsolescence are minimized.

Squeezing time out of a process, as we have said, is often the result of a series of small, prosaic steps that accumulate into an impressive gain. No company illustrates this better than manufacturer Tidel Engineering, Inc., where we implemented a number of improvements that reduced workers' ranges of motion on the job. The more limited the range of motion, as we saw in the case of the perambulating spoon factory employee, the faster the job gets done.

At Tidel, our process improvements began with a system of color coding the parts and bins that traveled down the assembly line. When the part appeared, we matched the color of the circuit boards with the same-colored containers. So, if the circuit board was green, all the parts for that board were in green containers. We had a separate person to refill the bins from which the line workers took the parts, so that they didn't have to get up.

The next level of improvement came when we noticed there was a lot of chatter among the bin filler and the line workers: "Hey, I need a part." Our solution was to place replacement bins directly behind the workers who used them, which accomplished two things: It cut the range of motion, and it reduced the number of lost parts.

Another manufacturer installed a micromotor on the conveyer belt so that we could vary the belt's speed in increments of micrometers per minute. This allowed management to increase output by speeding the pace at which people worked. If you do this gradually over a period of weeks, most workers don't notice that the belt is moving, say, one centimeter faster per minute than the day before. Those who do adjust usually find you may even implement this new process as a standard process. For example, new trainees begin work on "line B," which is the slowest one, then move to the faster "line A" after a few weeks.

Most manufacturers train some employees to handle five or six of the jobs on a line. These all-purpose replacement workers fill in at breaks. They never give a 15-minute break to the whole line at once. The line never stops.

Cost-Efficient Processes

Certain processes create inefficiencies and unnecessary expenses as they evolve. They may, for example, waste resources or consume too much time, but paying close attention to excesses can help squeeze out costs. Having a person or team permanently assigned to the task of finding cost-reducing OPIs, though an option beyond the resources of most companies, ensures an active, ongoing search.

Even if looking for OPIs is someone's ongoing, specific assignment, all employees should engage in the search. Rewarding good ideas will encourage creativity; furthermore, all thoughtful, well-intentioned suggestions, even if they don't work, should be recognized. In the optimal arrangement, a steady stream of fresh ideas is always percolating up from employees.

Cost-saving process changes can pop up virtually anywhere, from any source, for any activity: at the headquarters building (turn the heat off at night); at the factory (shorten the production line); at the distribution centers (buy smaller, easier-to-load trucks); for advertisers (plug two products with one ad); from unions (negotiate longer contracts); from resellers (combine two software products on the same disk); in packaging (remove the cardboard packing around CDs); with warranty relations (have consumers pay for shipping); or in product selection (reduce the number of colors offered).

Organizations need not continuously reinvent the wheel. Imitate the cost-saving process changes pioneered by other companies. Ideas such as product platforms, interchangeable product parts, and outsourcing are proven cost-reducing tactics. Others are more specific to the enterprise's own systems and structure. For example, a grocery store rotates new milk cartons to the back of the cooler to keep its stock fresh, or flight attendants sell duty-free goods during the long break between meals and arrival. The number of possible process variations is limited only by the imaginations of the people involved, who, if they remain cost conscious, will find that opportunities abound.

However, not every process change designed to reduce costs turns out as intended. Years ago, when the S&P Company's Schlitz Beer grew out of its capacity because its products were so successful, process engineers suggested speeding up the brewing system, thereby creating new capacity. The brewer very quickly adopted the new process, but the beer that resulted wasn't received as well by consumers. Schlitz reportedly didn't allow adequate time to test-market its new formula.

Product platforms (see Chapter 8) provide fertile ground for cost-saving process improvement. It is the nature of the beast: Platforms modify the product design process to incorporate existing ideas into future products. This convenient fit generates substantial cost savings that benefit consumers and, in addition, creates consumer value by expanding product selection. Although product platforms tend to spawn goods that aren't totally different from one another, consumers seem not to mind. The number of models available for purchase is the more compelling factor.

Another kind of process improvement maximizes the use of interchangeable parts in different models. Volkswagen AG's use of one chassis to make six car models is one example. Dell Computer Corporation makes use of the same concept when it offers countless model types that all fit into one of three outer shells. As part of a Phoenix Effect effort, a company reviews all of its products (including and especially those not yet in production) for cost-saving opportunities that derive from the use of interchangeable parts.

A third type of process change that reduces costs is outsourcing, which means moving the manufacture of

goods or the delivery of services to vendors who special-
ize in that particular work. Some organizations outsource
anything that isn't their forte. Circumventing tasks in
which they have no interest or aptitude frees them to
devote more time and resources to what they do best. All
companies outsource at some level, though they don't
always realize it. For example, a cereal maker may argue
that it doesn't outsource anything, but does it grow its
own wheat?

Automotive manufacturers generally utilize many suppliers. Generating purchase orders, verifying invoices, and
writing checks for so many vendors is a never-ending task.
To lighten its paperwork burden, industry leaders have
asked suppliers to incorporate parts into subassemblies
before shipping them. For example, dashboards, radios,
and knobs may be shipped separately. By authorizing the
dashboard maker to acquire and install the radios and
knobs, suppliers are reduced. This kind of modular assembly also provides outsourcing benefits, including fixed
delivery costs and a wider dispersion of responsibilities.
And, with several suppliers bidding for business, auto
assembly costs decline.

Cost-efficient processes have been standard operating
procedure at Wal-Mart Stores, Inc., since the company's
inception. Among the factors cited to explain its enormous
success are attention-getting prices, a friendly, down-
home culture, and the fact that, initially, its stores were
located away from their competition. But the sine qua non
of Wal-Mart's rise to the top is its mastery of the logistics
of procuring and distributing merchandise. By creating a
hub-and-spoke network, much like that used by major airlines, Wal-Mart fine-tunes its inventory levels and keeps its

costs below those of its competitors. The network operates by having a distribution center next to a major highway and positioning stores (Wal-Mart, Sam's Club, Wal-Mart Supercenters) within a one-day truck ride around that center. The sale of every item at each store is tracked from the center; the relevant information is communicated back to the manufacturer, making it possible for Wal-Mart to hold only minimal inventory. For example, in 2001 sales grew by 16 percent, while inventory grew by just 7 percent. Maintaining low inventory reduces the need for write-downs and markdowns, and the corporation saves money that would otherwise be spent moving boxes around. Wal-Mart's profits grew by 17 percent in 2001.

Quality-Efficient Processes

Back when Tidel Engineering was hitting bottom, customers were reporting huge quality problems. That is predictable when a company nearly goes out of business: You lose some or all of your best employees first.

One morning, it so happened that one of us was out in the warehouse when a truck backed up to unload a Tidel safe being returned from a customer. But the workers lost their grip and dropped the safe, slightly damaging it. Unfazed, the workers just picked up the safe and set it over to the side of the loading dock.

That afternoon we had a quality-control meeting. The head of manufacturing said there were issues that had to be discussed. He sent a new hire out to the warehouse to get a safe that 7-Eleven, Inc., one of the enterprise's biggest customers, had just returned. But the wrong safe was mistakenly wheeled back, and what we had was the unit that had fallen off the truck. For the next hour and a half, we discussed this safe as an example of the rough paint and poor quality issues facing the company. Due to the reports of quality-control problems, no one in the room found it remarkable that the safe was in such bad shape—in fact, looked as if it had been dropped.

Finally, at the end of the meeting, someone asked, "Are we sure this is the same safe we're having quality issues with?"—to which someone responded, "That's an interesting point, because it isn't the same model as the one we're discussing."

At that, everyone laughed, but bitterly; it was clear that our quality was so poor that we could not distinguish between a safe that had just fallen off a truck and a new one returned by the customer. Obviously, the painting, chipping, scraping, and packing issues were very serious. A thorough examination of all the relevant processes was most definitely called for.

Though it may be an amusing story, it has a powerful point: Returned, defective, and low-quality products are value destroyers and cause harm that takes considerable time and money to rectify. In addition, they shake the confidence and morale of everyone working for the business. Worst of all, bad products shatter the relationships between the company and its customers. Consumer choice is influenced primarily by brand and quality. In general, people buy strong, reputable brands, paying little attention to price or relative value, but with the assumption that the quality of the merchandise is high. Therefore, process improvements that enhance quality are critical.

Total quality management and Six Sigma are two approaches designed to improve processes and achieve higher-quality products. Both can be applied throughout the organization. While becoming a supplier of high-quality merchandise takes time, the first step is for all employees to concentrate on augmenting quality at every stage of business. Beginning with product design, the quality-enhancing process continues through factory configuration, inventory acquisition, assembly, distribution, sale, and postsale service.

But remember, from the perspective of the Phoenix Effect, a product can have too much quality. The right amount depends on how much consumers want to pay for it. Too much will drive them to less expensive choices. Six Sigma believes in uniform product quality, based on the assumption that customers who buy only small amounts of your product will judge it by its variance, rather than by its overall mean. Hence, consistency is paramount.

Most factories can correct manufacturing flaws, but fixing poor-quality designs is much harder. Designers trade off cost and quality because very few people will pay for an excessively expensive product, even if it is perfect.

Inventory purchases based solely on low cost can jeopardize quality; in fact, the total cost may increase when quality problems are addressed. Assembly, distribution, and sales efforts can come to nothing if employees mistreat semifinished goods, drop cartons, and conduct installations improperly, all of which diminish quality and disappoint customers. One model for improving quality comes from *kaizen,* or "continuous improvement," the Japanese management technique we discussed earlier in the context of Westinghouse Air Brake. *Kaizen* modifies factory configurations by ceaselessly tweaking processes to improve their quality and obtain cost efficiencies.

Quality standards develop out of corporate culture. The strategic decisions made by executives and managers—and how those decisions are executed—determine if quality is high or low. If a culture, which moves from the top down, accepts sluggish performance, then it sanctions poor quality. Pursuing and maintaining high quality is a perpetual process; once lost, a reputation for quality can be very hard to regain.

In 1994, US Airways Group, Inc.'s US Airways was perceived to have a problem with quality, which is the same thing as having one in most industries. Within a short period, three of its planes crashed—at a time when the rest of the industry remained accident free. Staggered by these disasters, US Airways hired a new chief of aircraft safety and engineering to whom it gave an ample budget. It took time, but gradually the organization overcame public mistrust, and in 1999 it was awarded the number one position in airline quality. Anything short of a dramatic response would have risked US Airways very existence; it might have suffered the same fate as ValuJet Airlines, Inc., which never recovered from the terrible plunge of one of its aircraft into a Florida swamp in 1996.

No process is more quality efficient than the one that made Michael Dell. Called "mass customization," Dell Computer Corporation's system of built-to-order manufacturing shortens the supply chain and, by minimizing its inventory, protects the company against obsolescence. In an industry in which 10 to 15 percent of equipment remains unsold, Dell's percentage of written-off or marked-down merchandise is substantially lower. It is no wonder that Dell's competitors (such as Compaq Computer Corporation), as well as companies outside the computer industry, such as Gerber Scientific, Inc., are following Dell's lead in custom building products to buyers' specifications.

Dell's method looked like it could be the answer for Koss Corporation, a maker of stereo headphones, which, in addition, licenses its name to other manufacturers of electronic goods. After emerging from bankruptcy in 1986, Koss initiated built-to-order manufacturing. It soon became apparent, however, that there were important differences between Dell and Koss. One problem was that Koss's orders came all at once during holiday seasons, when the labor market was tight, forcing Koss to hire workers from temporary employment agencies to get through the rush. As a result, far too many orders were left unfilled, while many that were met consisted of inferior products that were returned after the holidays. Further complicating the process for Koss was that, unlike Dell, it doesn't sell to end users; it supplies retail outlets, and some pressured the company into assuming additional work, like packing and product mixing. Moreover, Koss's equipment doesn't become obsolete nearly as rapidly as Dell's computers do. Consequently, low inventory isn't the advantage it is to Dell, and at times, it actually prevented Koss from filling a number of big orders.

As a result, Koss eventually abandoned the built-to-order idea. It accumulated inventory, fired its temporary workers and the less reliable second shift, and rearranged its manufacturing operations so that all 80 of its products could be assembled on any production line. These changes advanced deliveries from several weeks to two days, enabling Koss to accept large unexpected orders; the modifications reduced costs and improved quality. The lesson to learn here is this: Never assume that an innovation that works for another company will automatically work for yours.

The Product Makes the Process

Processes aren't an abstract concept. Their value is determined by the value of the product they work to create. Whether a process is useful depends on the success of the goods or services that reach the consumer. This interconnectedness leads us to two practical suggestions with which we will close the chapter.

First, you can't evaluate your own processes without being thoroughly familiar with your competitors' products. The best way to do that is to go shopping and buy them right off the shelf. Check to see if your competitors remembered to include instructions.

Then, bring those products into your office or plant and test them on a panel of customers. Use independent people who have no ties to your company and who represent the market for which the product was designed. Don't involve your own employees. Place your competitors' products alongside your own and ask each person to rank them and to discuss the advantages and disadvantages of each. Depending on your products, this could take an hour or a few days.

Second, and even more important, listen to your customers. You will find them full of ideas about your product—how and where it is sold, its packaging, and its price.

Their insights can help you redesign and improve your processes significantly. An organization that doesn't log its customers' comments and complaints has an incomplete quality process. You can't start authentic process improvement until you understand how, according to your customers, your products stack up against those of your competitors.

Epilogue

Like a lifetime Maalox Moment, many of us recall that indelible day when some officious schoolteacher gravely informed our parents that we weren't working at capacity or living up to our potential. Some of us recall whole years when that is *all* anyone had to say about us. However unwelcome, the news was usually true—just as it is for hundreds of underperforming U.S. companies that face a choice of either revitalizing themselves or sliding further down the slippery slope to oblivion.

Fortunately, the choice is both clear and easy to carry out. When the novelist F. Scott Fitzgerald famously wrote, "There are no second acts in American lives," he was famously wrong. This whole country is a metaphor for second chances. Built on comebacks, it is the one culture where failures nearly always get another crack at success, providing they display the savvy and the spirit needed to get off the canvas and start swinging again.

That's the premise of this book: Never say never. Readers of these 10 chapters will have no doubt about our own faith in the power of renewal, exemplified by the success of business transformation techniques that we have spent decades acquiring and applying to all kinds of companies. *The Phoenix Effect* is a testament to what has worked for scores of others, and it will surely work for you. We dedicate this manual of business self-renewal to all those who showed us how to show you the way back. Most of all, we dedicate it to your own company's revitalization.

They made it; you will, too.

Sources and
Suggested Reading

INTRODUCTION

Sources for material on the phoenix myth include Mary R. Lefkowitz, "phoenix," World Book Online Americas Edition, www.aolsvc. worldbook.aol.com; www.pantheon.org; *The Columbia Encyclopedia*, 6th ed., "phoenix."

CHAPTER 1

Sources for material on NeoStar, Inc., include "The Week In Business," *The Dallas Business Journal*, December 9, 1996; Cheryl Hall, "Space-Time Continuum," *The Dallas Morning News*, May 21, 2000, p. H1.

Sources for material on Cendant Corporation include Amy Barrett, with Stephanie Anderson Forest and Tom Lowry, "Henry Silverman's Long Road Back," *Business Week*, February 28, 2000, p. 126; "Cendant Audit Finds Falsifications at CUC," *The Washington Post*, August 28, 1998, p. F1; David J. Morrow, "Cendant Finds $115 Million Account Error," *The New York Times*, April 16, 1998, p. D1; "Cendant Reports Accounting Error," *Facts on File World News Digest*, April 23, 1998, p. E1; www.hoovers.com.

CHAPTER **2**

Sources for material on Tidel Engineering, Inc., include "Tidel Engineering Obtains $1.6 Million Southland Corporation Contract," *PR Newswire,* April 14, 1993.

Sources for material on Palm, Inc., include Ian Fried, "Stock Market Gives Palm a Thumbs-Down," www.news.cnet.com, December 21, 2000.

Sources for material on *The Wonder Boys* film include www.wonder boys.com.

Sources for the material on Uno Restaurant Corporation include David Farkas, "Bound for the Burbs," *Chain Leader,* June 2000, pp. 45–50; www.hoovers.com.

Source for material on the Jaguar division of the Ford Motor Company: Dan Neil, "Behind the Wheel/2002 Jaguar X-Type," *The New York Times,* August 19, 2001, sec. 12, p. 1.

Sources for material on SyQuest Technology, Inc., include "SyQuest Technology Announces Name Change," *Business Wire,* April 22, 1999.

Sources for material on Venator Group, Inc., include Rachel Beck, "Venator Sells German Chain," Associated Press, September 22, 1998; www.venator.com; www.hoovers.com.

Sources for material on Bertelsmann AG include David D. Kirkpatrick, "A Reshuffling at an Online Bookseller," *The New York Times,* May 17, 2001, p. C6.

Sources for material on Liz Claiborne, Inc., include Teri Agins, "How Liz Claiborne Became Fashion's P&G," *The Wall Street Journal,* February 2, 2000, p. B1; www.hoovers.com; www.lizclaiborne.com.

Sources for material on Thermo Electron Corporation include www.thermo.com; www.hoovers.com.

Sources for material on Oakley, Inc., include www.hoovers.com.

Sources for material on the Mayo Clinic include www.mayo clinic.com.

Sources for material on Drury Inn, Inc., include www.drury-inn.com.

Sources for material on The Premcor Refining Group, Inc., include www.hoovers.com; www.premcorinc.com.

Source for material on Steinway & Sons: Beth Gardiner, "Steinway & Sons Still Making Its Fine Sounds," *Chicago Tribune,* January 21, 1999, p. C8.

CHAPTER 3

Sources for material on Sun TV & Appliance, Inc., and H. H. Gregg Appliances & Electronics Co. include Mark Williams, "Indianapolis Electronics Chain to Lease Six Old Sun TV Stores," The Associated Press, April 14, 1999; www.hoovers.com; www.hhgregg.com.

Sources for material on Laura Ashley Holdings, PLC, include www.hoovers.com.

Sources for material on Ameritrade, Inc., include "E-News," *The Detroit News*, October 4, 2000; Rebecca Buckman, "Ameritrade Stumbles in Pursuing Web Turf," *The Wall Street Journal*, October 26, 1998; www.hoovers.com.

Sources for material on OTASCO, Inc., include Teresa McUsic, "Otasco Will Rise Again, Chairman Says," *Tulsa World*, November 8, 1998, p. A1; "OTASCO Goes Bankrupt; Shutters 170 Stores, Lays Off 1,600," *Automotive Marketing*, December 1988, p. 12.

CHAPTER 4

Sources for material on Best Buy Co. include Evan Ramstad, "Best Buy Co. Is Stacking the Shelves to Add to Profit," *The Wall Street Journal*, April 28, 1999, p. B4; Chris Dettro, "Best Buy Opening New Store Today," *The State Journal-Register*, June 23, 1995, p. 12.

Sources for material on Circuit City Stores, Inc., include www.hoovers.com.

Sources for material on Clear Channel Communications, Inc., include Maureen Dezell and Steve Morse, "Radio Giant Clear Channel Buys SFX," *The Boston Globe*, March 1, 2000, p. F2; Stuart Elliott, "Clear Channel in $3 Billion Deal to Acquire SFX Entertainment," *The New York Times*, March 1, 2000, p. C1; www.hoovers.com.

Sources for material on Yahoo!, Inc., include Kara Swisher, "Yahoo's Quarter Net Tops Expectations," *The Wall Street Journal*, October 8, 1998, p. B5; www.hoovers.com.

Sources for material on AT&T Corporation include Steve Raabe, "Malone Setting Sights on AT&T," *The Denver Post*, August 17, 2000, p. C1.

Sources for material on CDNow, Inc., and NK2, Inc., include Judith Messina and Mark Walsh, "Former N2K Staffers Flood Alley," *Crain's New York Business*, March 29, 1999, p. 12.

Sources for material on Boston Market Corporation include Michael Arndt, "There's Life Left in the Old Bird Yet," *Business Week*, May 14, 2001, pp. 77–78; www.hoovers.com; www.bostonmarket.com.

CHAPTER 5

Sources for material on EEX Corporation include www.eex.com.

Source for material on Northeast Utilities Services Company: "Northeast Utilities, Connecticut Light & Power and Western Massachusetts Electric Co. Ratings Raised by Fitch IBCA," *PR Newswire*, March 23, 1999.

Sources for material on Netscape Communications Corporation and Infoseek Corporation include "Infoseek Renegotiates Deal with Netscape," *The New York Times*, November 28, 1998, p. C15; www.hoovers.com.

Sources for material on Kia Motors Co., Ltd., include Lee Kap-Soo, "Kia Creditors Set to Write Off Debts to Make Second Auction Success," *The Korea Herald*, September 10, 1998; Keith Naughton, with Karen Lowry Miller and Joann Muller, "The Global Six," *Business Week*, International Edition, January 25, 1999, p. 16; Oles Gadacz, "More Daewoo Disarray," *Automotive News*, November 8, 1999, p. 3; www.hoovers.com.

Sources for material on Business Express Airlines and AMR Corporation's American Airlines include Jerry Ackerman, "American Airlines Unit to Buy Business Express," *The Boston Globe*, December 5, 1998, p. F1; www.hoovers.com; www.amr.com.

Sources for material on BankBoston Corporation and BayBanks, Inc., include Lynn Arditi, "Fleet Reshuffling Takes Shape," *Providence Journal-Bulletin*, October 13, 1998, p. G2; Liz Moyer, "Fleet and BankBoston Pick Transition Team," *The American Banker*, April 5, 1999, p. 32.

Sources for material on the Clayton Antitrust Act include Neal R. Stoll and Shepard Goldfein, "Changing Competitive Landscape," *New York Law Journal*, June 18, 1996, p. 3.

CHAPTER 6

Sources for material on Louis Pasteur quote include *Investor's Business Daily*, March 29, 2001, p. A3.

Sources for material on the American Express Company include www.americanexpress.com.

Sources for material on Visa International, Inc., include www.visa.com.

Sources for material on Willie Sutton include "Famous Cases, Willie Sutton," www.fbi.gov.

Source for material on Exxon Mobil Corporation's Speedpass: "Exxon Mobil Expands the Speedpass System to More Than 2,500 Exxon-Branded Service Stations," *News Release*, August 1, 2001, www.exxon.mobil.com.

Sources for material on the paper industry include www.inter nationalpaper.com.

CHAPTER 7

Sources for material on RadioShack Corporation include Cade Metz, "RadioShack, Compaq Presario 5070 Company Business and Marketing," *PC Magazine*, September 1, 1999, p. 191; Laura Heller, "RadioShack 'Reinvents' Style, Takes Connectivity to Tucson," *DSN Retailing Today*, November 20, 2000, p. 1.

Sources for material on Tricon Global Restaurants, Inc., include Richard Gibson, "Tricon Is Serving Up a Fast-Food Turnaround," *The Wall Street Journal*, February 11, 1999, p. B10; www.bigcharts.com.

Sources for material on Edison Schools, Inc., include Tamar Lewin, "Edison Schools Say Students Gain," *The New York Times*, April 7, 1999, p. B9; www.hoovers.com.

Sources for material on Delta Air Lines, Inc., and America West Holdings Corporation include Martha Brannigan, "Delta Air Lines Wrestles with Discontent among Pilots," *The Wall Street Journal*, October 12, 1998, p. B4; Martha Brannigan, "Pilots Keep Delta CEO Hopping," *The Desert News*, April 24, 2001, p. A1; Peter Corbett, "AMWEST, Pilots Again Talking New Contract," *The Arizona Republic*, March 2, 2000, p. D1; Dave Hirschman, "Delta Air Lines Pilots Explain Reasons for Possible Strike," *Atlanta Journal and Constitution*, March 3, 2001; Scott McCartney, "America West Contract War Is Over More Than Money," *The Wall Street Journal*, March 8, 1999, p. B4; Scott Thurston, "Delta Pilots Approve Pay Scale on New 737," *The Atlanta Journal and Constitution*, October 17, 1998, p. E1.

Sources for material on OTASCO, Inc., include Teresa McUsic, "Otasco Will Rise Again, Chairman Says," *Tulsa World*, November 8, 1998, p. A1; "OTASCO Goes Bankrupt," *Automotive Marketing*, December 1988, p. 12.

CHAPTER 8

Sources for material on Fred's, Inc., include Laurel Campbell, "Fred's Moving Back to Dollar-Store Roots," *The Commercial Appeal*, August 19, 1995, p. 4B; Dewanna Lofton, "Shopping—Fred's Stores Are Telling the Big Boys to Make Room," *The Commercial Appeal*, June 18, 1998, p. 4B.

Sources for material on Hasbro, Inc., and Mattel, Inc., include Joseph Pereira, "Toys: Hasbro Strikes Back," *The Wall Street Journal*, April 15, 1999, p. B1.

Sources for material on The Home Depot, Inc., include James R. Hagerty, "Home Depot's New Advice for Do-It-Yourselfers," *The Wall Street Journal*, October 19, 1998, p. B1; www.homedepot.com.

Sources for material on McDonald's Corporation include James P. Miller, "Did Somebody Say Pizza? McDonald's Agrees to Acquire Midwestern Chain," *The Wall Street Journal*, May 6, 1999, p. A4; Margaret Studer and Jeffiner Ordonez, "The Golden Arches, Burgers, Fries and 4-Star Rooms," *The Wall Street Journal*, November 17, 2000, p. B1; www.mcdonalds.com.

Sources for material on Sun Country Airlines include "Sun Country Applauds Other Airlines for Finally Doing the Right Thing for Customers," *PR Newswire*, December 15, 1999; Susan Carey, "Charter Airline Sun Country to Become Scheduled Carrier in Big Strategy Shift," *The Wall Street Journal*, January 18, 1999; Kristin Miller, Sun Country Airlines press release, December 15, 1999.

Sources for material on the Ford Motor Company include Robert L. Simison, "Ford Hopes Its New Focus Will Be a Global Bestseller," *The Wall Street Journal*, October 8, 1998, p. B10.

Sources for material on Volkswagen AG and Nissan Motor Company, Ltd., include Michelle Krebs, "From One Platform Many Models Grow," *The New York Times*, May 19, 1999, p. G7; "Renault and Nissan Renissant?" *The Economist*, March 20, 1999, p. 65.

Sources for material on Sony Corporation include "Sony Spins Another Small Wonder," *The Des Moines Register*, May 19, 1999, p. 6; Karen Gines and Rachel L. Fox, "Electronic Awards," *Incentive*, June 1999, pp. A1–A8; Peter Landers, "Sony Announces New CD Player with Better Sound," *The Wall Street Journal*, April 7, 1999, p. B4.

Sources for material on Revlon, Inc., include Emily Nelson, "Revlon Planning Another Makeover," *The Arizona Republic*, November 26, 2000, p. D1.

Sources for material on Starbucks Corporation include Nelson D. Schwartz, "Still Perking after All These Years," *Fortune*, May 24, 1999, p. 203; www.hoovers.com.

Sources for material on Pets.com, Inc., include Dan McGraw, "There Was Just No Appetite for Online Dog Food," *U.S. News & World Report*, November 20, 2000, p. 74.

Sources for material on The Stop & Shop Companies, Inc., include Nora Lockwood Tooher, "Rhode Island Supermarket Chain Raises the Stakes in the Discount Card Arena," *Providence Journal-Bulletin*, October 22, 2000.

Sources for material on Charles Hofer include C. W. Hofer, "Conceptual Constructs for Formulating Corporate and Business Strategies," no. 9-378-754, Intercollegiate Case Clearing House, Boston, 1977.

Sources for material on The Gillette Company include Dana Canedy, "Gillette to Cut Jobs by 11 Percent As Results Lag," *The New York Times*, September 29, 1998, p. C1.

Sources for material on Polaroid Corporation include Elkan Blout, "Polaroid Dreams to Reality," *Daedalus*, March 22, 1996, p. 39.

Sources for material on United Technology Corporation's Pratt & Whitney include "Gently Down Stream," *Airline Business*, October 1997, p. 52.

Sources for material on eMachines, Inc., include "Digits," *The Wall Street Journal*, December 3, 1998, p. B6; Jane Turnis, "Established Internet Providers Offer Free Access for Commitment," *The Gazette* (Colorado Springs, CO), March 5, 2000.

Sources for material on the Hewlett-Packard Company include Eric Nee, "Open Season on Carly Fiorina," *Fortune*, July 23, 2001, p. 114.

Sources for material on the airline industry include Roger E. Bilstein, "Wright Brothers," World Book Online Americas Edition, www.aol.com; Ed Perkins, "Low-Fare Airlines Deserve Protection from Big Guys," *The Orlando Sentinel*, July 28, 1998, p. L2.

Sources for material on Ameritrade, Inc., include "E-News," *The Detroit News*, October 4, 2000; Rebecca Buckman, "Ameritrade

Stumbles in Pursuing Web Turf," *The Wall Street Journal*, October 26, 1998; www.hoovers.com.

Sources for material on airline pricing include Steve Huettel, "Click and Fly," *St. Petersburg Times*, June 25, 2001, p. E11.

Sources for material on Southwest Airlines, Inc., include Bill Morrison, "Southwest Airlines Expands Here," *St. Louis Business Journal*, March 27, 1989, p. B8.

CHAPTER **9**

Sources for material on Pathmark Stores, Inc., include Ericka Blount, "Food Fight in Brooklyn," *The Wall Street Journal*, October 21, 1998, p. B22.

Sources for material on the Burger King Corporation include Richard Gibson, "Burger King Seeks New Sizzle," *The Wall Street Journal*, April 14, 1999, p. B1; www.hoovers.com.

Sources for material on the Toyota Motor Company include Lisa Shuchman, "Toyota Revamps Plants for Shift to Exports If Local Markets Fail," *The Wall Street Journal*, October 7, 1998, p. A17.

Sources for material on GC Companies, Inc.'s, General Cinema include Bruce Horovitz, "Butter on Your Trail Mix?" *Los Angeles Times*, July 20, 1993, p. D1.

Sources for material on Concentric Network Corporation include Joseph Menn and Greg Miller, "How a Visionary Venture on the Web Unraveled," *Los Angeles Times*, May 7, 2000, p. A1.

Sources for material on FedEx Corporation include Douglas A. Blackmon, "FedEx Makes Plans to Alter Its Operations," *The Wall Street Journal*, November 11, 1998, p. A3; Ann Saccomano, "FPA Mails Ballots to FedEx Pilots," *Traffic World*, January 11, 1999, p. 23.

Sources for material on Leslie Kaufman include "Fingerhut Gives Federated Edge in E-Commerce," *The New York Times*, July 6, 1999, p. C1; Emily Nelson, "Wal-Mart Turns to Books-A-Million to Supply Books for Web Site," *The Wall Street Journal*, July 2, 1999, p. A3; www.hoovers.com.

CHAPTER **10**

Sources for material on the Westinghouse Air Brake Company include Timothy Aeppel, "More, More, More—Rust Belt Factory Lifts Productivity," *The Wall Street Journal*, May 18, 1999, p. A1.

Sources for material on Volkswagen AG include Michelle Krebs, "From One Platform Many Models Grow," *The New York Times*, May 19, 1999, p. G7.

Sources for material on General Motors Corporation include Jeffrey Ball, "UAW Chief Blasts GM's Modular-Assembly Plan," *The Wall Street Journal*, March 29, 1999, p. A2.

Sources for material on Wal-Mart Stores, Inc., include Jean Kinsey, "A Faster, Leaner, Supply Chain," *American Journal of Agricultural Economics*, November 15, 2000, p. 1123; Emily Nelson, "Logistics Whiz Rises at Wal-Mart," *The Wall Street Journal*, March 11, 1999, p. B1; www.hoovers.com.

Sources for material on management techniques include Carnegie Library's Business Librarians, "Concepts Of Six Sigma, Easy to Understand with Book," *Pittsburgh Post-Gazette*, August 26, 2001, p. C2; Bob Quick, "A Brilliant Success," *The Santa Fe New Mexican*, May 27, 2001, p. D1; Nanda Majumdar and Rakhi Mazumdar, "TCM & TQM—TCM the TQM Way," *Business Today*, January 7, 1999, p. 60.

Sources for material on US Airways, Inc., include "Jittery Charlotte Tries to Make Plans beyond USAir," *Roanoke Times & World News*, December 30, 1994, p. A7; Glen Johnson, "U.S. Airways Places First in Quality Survey," *The Associated Press News Wire*, April 20, 1999; Rob Zaleski, "Air Crash Proves There's No Value in $49 Ticket," *Capital Times* (Madison, WI), December 2, 1996, p. D1.

Sources for material on Dell Computer Corporation include Diane Brady et al., "Customizing for the Masses," *Business Week*, March 20, 2000, p. 130; J. William Gurley and Jane Hodges, "A Dell for Every Industry," *Fortune*, October 12, 1998, p. 167; Gary Williams, "Computers—Mimicking Dell, Compaq to Sell Its PCs Directly," *The Wall Street Journal*, November 11, 1998, p. B1.

Sources for material on Koss Corporation include Evan Ramstad, "Koss CEO Gambles on Inventory Buildup," *The Wall Street Journal*, March 15, 1999, section B, p. 7A.

EPILOGUE

Sources for F. Scott Fitzgerald quote include John Greenwald, "Peterman Reboots," *Time*, August 20, 2001, p. Y3.

Index